✧ *Companions for the Journey* ✧

Praying with
Vincent de Paul

✧ *Companions for the Journey* ✧

Praying with
Vincent de Paul

by
Thomas McKenna, CM

Saint Mary's Press
Christian Brothers Publications
Winona, Minnesota

✧ *To my parents, Grace and Gene McKenna,* ✧
who would have been Vincent's good friends, had they met.
All three knew the meaning of practical love and recognized
its source in the love of Jesus Christ.

The publishing team for this book included Carl Koch, FSC, development editor; Joellen Barak Ramer, manuscript editor; Maura C. Goessling, typesetter; Elaine Kohner, illustrator; pre-press, printing, and binding by the graphics division of Saint Mary's Press.

The acknowledgments continue on page 115.

Printed in the United States of America.

Printing: 9 8 7 6 5 4 3 2 1

Year: 2002 01 00 1999 98 97 96 95 94

ISBN 0-88489-316-2

✧ Contents ✧

✧ Foreword ✧

Companions for the Journey

Just as food is required for human life, so are companions. Indeed, the word *companions* comes from two Latin words: *com*, meaning "with," and *panis*, meaning "bread." Companions nourish our heart, mind, soul, and body. They are also the people with whom we can celebrate the sharing of bread.

Perhaps the most touching stories in the Bible are about companionship: the Last Supper, the wedding feast at Cana, the sharing of the loaves and the fishes, and Jesus' breaking of bread with the disciples on the road to Emmaus. Each incident of companionship with Jesus revealed more about his mercy, love, wisdom, suffering, and hope. When Jesus went to pray in the Garden of Olives, he craved the companionship of the Apostles. They let him down. But God sent the Spirit to inflame the hearts of the Apostles, and they became faithful companions to Jesus and to one another.

Throughout history, other faithful companions have followed Jesus and the Apostles. These saints and mystics have also taken the journey from conversion, through suffering, to resurrection. Just as they were inspired by the holy people who went before them, so too may you take them as your companions as you walk on your spiritual journey.

The Companions for the Journey series is a response to the spiritual hunger of Christians. This series makes available the rich spiritual teachings of mystics and guides whose wisdom can help us on our pilgrimages. As you complete the last meditation in each volume, it is hoped that you will feel supported, challenged, and affirmed by a soul-companion on your spiritual journey.

The spiritual hunger that has emerged over the last twenty years is a great sign of renewal in Christian life. People fill retreat programs and workshops on topics in spirituality. The demand for spiritual directors exceeds the number available. Interest in the lives and writings of saints and mystics is increasing as people search for models of whole and holy Christian life.

Praying with Vincent de Paul

Praying with Vincent de Paul is more than just a book about Vincent's spirituality. This book seeks to engage you in praying in the way that Vincent did about issues and themes that were central to his experience. Each meditation can enlighten your understanding of his spirituality and lead you to reflect on your own experience.

The goal of *Praying with Vincent de Paul* is that you will discover Vincent's rich spirituality and integrate his spirit and wisdom into your relationship with God, with your brothers and sisters, and with your own heart and mind.

Suggestions for Praying with Vincent de Paul

Meet Vincent, a fascinating companion for your pilgrimage, by reading the introduction to this book, which begins on page 13. It provides a brief biography of Vincent and an outline of the major themes of his spirituality.

Once you meet Vincent, you will be ready to pray with him and to encounter God, your sisters and brothers, and yourself in new and wonderful ways. To help your prayer, here are some suggestions that have been part of the tradition of Christian spirituality:

Create a sacred space. Jesus said, "'When you pray, go to your private room, shut yourself in, and so pray to your [God] who is in that secret place, and your [God] who sees all that is done in secret will reward you'" (Matthew 6:6). Solitary prayer is best done in a place where you can have privacy and silence, both of which can be luxuries in the life of busy people. If privacy and silence are not possible, create a quiet, safe place within yourself, perhaps while riding to and from work, while sitting in line at the dentist's office, or while waiting for someone. Do the best you can, knowing that a loving God is present everywhere. Whether the meditations in this book are used for solitary prayer or with a group, try to create a prayerful mood with candles, meditative music, an open Bible, or a crucifix.

Open yourself to the power of prayer. Every human experience has a religious dimension. All of life is suffused with God's presence. So remind yourself that God is present as you begin your period of prayer. Do not worry about distractions. If something keeps intruding during your prayer, spend some time talking with God about it. Be flexible because God's Spirit blows where it will.

Prayer can open your mind and widen your vision. Be open to new ways of seeing God, people, and yourself. As you open yourself to the Spirit of God, different emotions are evoked, such as sadness from tender memories, or joy from a celebration recalled. Our emotions are messages from God that can tell us much about our spiritual quest. Also, prayer strengthens our will to act. Through prayer, God can touch our will and empower us to live according to what we know is true.

Finally, many of the meditations in this book will call you to employ your memories, your imagination, and the circumstances of your life as subjects for prayer. The great mystics and saints realized that they had to use all their resources to know God better. Indeed, God speaks to us continually and touches us constantly. We must learn to listen and feel with all the means that God has given us.

Come to prayer with an open mind, heart, and will.

Preview each meditation before beginning. After you have placed yourself in God's presence, spend a few moments previewing the readings and especially the reflection activities. Several reflection activities are given in each meditation because different styles of prayer appeal to different personalities or personal needs. **Note that each meditation has more**

reflection activities than can be done during one prayer period. Therefore, select only one or two reflection activities each time you use a meditation. Do not feel compelled to complete all the reflection activities.

Read meditatively. Each meditation offers you a story about Vincent and a reading from his writings. Take your time reading. If a particular phrase touches you, stay with it. Relish its feelings, meanings, and concerns.

Use the reflections. Following the readings is a short reflection in commentary form, which is meant to give perspective to the readings. Then you are offered several ways of meditating on the readings and the theme of the prayer. You may be familiar with the different methods of meditating, but in case you are not, they are described briefly here:

✦ *Repeated short prayer or mantra:* One means of focusing your prayer is to use a mantra, or "prayer word." The mantra may be a single word or a short phrase taken from the readings or from the Scriptures. For example, a short prayer for meditation 1 in this book is simply the phrase "loving God." Repeated slowly in harmony with your breathing, the mantra helps you center your heart and mind on one action or attribute of God.

✦ *Lectio divina:* This type of meditation is "divine studying," a concentrated reflection on the word of God or the wisdom of a spiritual writer. Most often in *lectio divina,* you will be invited to read one of the passages several times and then concentrate on one or two sentences, pondering their meaning for you and their effect on you. *Lectio divina* commonly ends with formulation of a resolution.

✦ *Guided meditation:* In this type of meditation, our imagination helps us consider alternative actions and likely consequences. Our imagination helps us experience new ways of seeing God, our neighbors, ourselves, and nature. When Jesus told his followers parables and stories, he engaged their imagination. In this book, you will be invited to follow guided meditations.

One way of doing a guided meditation is to read the scene or story several times, until you know the outline and can recall it when you enter into reflection. Or before your prayer time, you may wish to record the meditation on a tape recorder. If so, remember to allow pauses for reflection between phrases and to speak with a slow, peaceful pace and tone. Then, during prayer, when you have finished the readings and the reflection commentary, you can turn on your recording of the meditation and be led through it. If you find your own voice too distracting, ask a friend to make the tape for you.

✦ *Examen of consciousness:* The reflections often will ask you to examine how God has been speaking to you in your past and present experience—in other words, the reflections will ask you to examine your awareness of God's presence in your life.

✦ *Journal writing:* Writing is a process of discovery. If you write for any length of time, stating honestly what is on your mind and in your heart, you will unearth much about who you are, how you stand with your God, what deep longings reside in your soul, and more. In some reflections, you will be asked to write a dialog with Jesus or someone else. If you have never used writing as a means of meditation, try it. Reserve a special notebook for your journal writing. If desired, you can go back to your entries at a future time for an examen of consciousness.

✦ *Action:* Occasionally, a reflection will suggest singing a favorite hymn, going out for a walk, or undertaking some other physical activity. Action, particularly service, can be a meaningful form of prayer.

Using the Meditations for Group Prayer

If you wish to use the meditations for community prayer, these suggestions may help:

✦ Read the theme to the group. Call the community into the presence of God, using the short opening prayer. Invite one or two participants to read one or both readings. If you use both readings, observe the pause between them.

✦ The reflection commentary may be used as a reading, or it can be deleted, depending on the needs and interests of the group.

✦ Select one of the reflection activities for your group. Allow sufficient time for your group to reflect, to recite a centering prayer or mantra, to accomplish a studying prayer (*lectio divina*), or to finish an examen of consciousness. Depending on the group and the amount of available time, you may want to invite the participants to share their reflections, responses, or petitions with the group.

✦ Reading the passage from the Scriptures may serve as a summary of the meditation.

✦ If a formulated prayer or a psalm is given as a closing, it may be recited by the entire group. Or you may ask participants to offer their own prayers for the closing.

Now you are ready to begin praying with Vincent de Paul, a faithful and caring companion on this stage of your spiritual journey. It is hoped that you will find him to be a true soul-companion.

CARL KOCH, FSC
Editor

Note: The author has made a modern translation of many of the letters and documents of Vincent that have been used in this book. The original collection in French is Pierre Coste's fourteen volume collection, *Saint Vincent de Paul: Correspondence, Entretiens, Documents*. Father McKenna's translation is cited as *Documents*.

✧ Introduction ✧

The Attraction of Vincent

"To love another person is to see the face of God." This arresting line from the musical version of *Les Misérables* summarizes rather well the spirituality of Vincent de Paul, who lived two centuries before the novel was written. Although Vincent was a spiritual director of diocesan priests, a peasant on intimate terms with nobility, part of the vanguard of a wave of Church renewal, a creative genius at organizing social welfare programs, and a master preacher, he was most of all a person who found and served God in the *anawim*, the poor, sick, abandoned outcasts in the countryside and the city.

Vincent drew other people into his projects and made them his co-workers. Many priests and laymen joined him, but he broke new ground by inviting women to serve poor and sick people out in society. The Daughters of Charity lived and worked outside of cloisters, a dramatic change for women religious. Today worldwide, many women and men follow in Vincent's footsteps as members of the Congregation of the Mission (Vincentians), the Daughters of Charity, the Vincent de Paul Society, parish welfare associations, and Catholic charity operations.

His gift for integrating service with a profound life of prayer is one of Vincent's greatest attractions to contemporary Christians. Vincent's mix of praying and doing has appealed to tens of thousands of believers over the last three centuries. He is still a valued spiritual companion for people who

✦ struggle to integrate prayer and meditation with service to their needy neighbor;

✦ become spiritually exhausted by their activity instead of being nourished by it;

✦ have seen God in the eyes of poor, sick, homeless, despairing people.

Vincent will be a good companion to anyone who seeks balance between action and contemplation, organizing good works and relying on divine providence, intelligent activity and trusting surrender. He learned this balance in the crucible of his own wide experience, as can be seen in his story.

Vincent's Story

Vincent lived during one of the most spiritually and apostolically fertile periods in European history. A visible part of the Counter-Reformation ferment, Vincent joined with a number of other remarkable personalities in France who changed the religious face of the country in the space of one generation.

Early Life

Vincent was born in 1581 into a farming family at Puoy, in the southeastern corner of France. Like other small acreage peasants, Jean and Bertrande Paul struggled, but they managed better than most to keep food on the table for their six children. They even had the resources to send their bright second son, Vincent, to a local school—as an investment in their own future as well as his.

Loved as a child and especially close to his mother, Vincent hoped to rise in the world and come back as the family's pride and provider. A well-to-do townsman spotted Vincent's talent and sent him on for further studies. Devoted, but certainly not extraordinarily so, Vincent set his sights on the priesthood. In sixteenth-century French society, priesthood was not necessarily a fast track to fortune, but it was a common enough one.

Vincent studied in Toulouse and, even though the Council of Trent decreed that no one should be ordained before age twenty-five, Vincent received Holy Orders at nineteen. He concealed his true age and found an elderly bishop to perform the service. Vincent immediately set out to make his way in the world. Interestingly, in later years, Vincent never spoke of this period of his life.

Two Years Shrouded in Mystery

To support himself while studying, Vincent ran a small boarding school. Even though the school seemed to thrive, Vincent's debts mounted. He could not secure appointment to a parish, despite much effort.

At this point, a generous woman from Toulouse remembered him in her will, but a complication arose. To get the inheritance, Vincent had to go after a man who owed money to the woman. This shifty debtor had run off to Marseilles. Anxious to recoup the money, Vincent leased a horse and took off after him. Along the way, Vincent's money ran out, so he sold his rented horse to tide him over. When Vincent found the debtor, he had the man thrown into prison and before long obtained his inheritance. To economize on the trip back home, Vincent booked passage on a ship heading across the Mediterranean to his part of France. What actually happened to him after this, between 1605 and 1607, remains the subject of considerable speculation. Perhaps he was just hiding from his creditors, but he virtually disappeared for two years.

A legend grew that he had been captured by pirates. This story had its basis in letters Vincent wrote to a benefactor soon after he returned to France. According to his story, the pirates sold him into slavery in Tunis. After serving under a fisherman, then a chemist-magician, and finally a farmer, Vincent managed to escape in a small boat with his last owner, an apostate from Christianity who wanted to be rejoined to his faith. They sailed across hundreds of miles of open sea to safety in southern France.

The two having made their way to Avignon, Vincent, as the valiant rescuer, caught the attention of the papal vice-legate. Vincent said in a letter: "He does me the honour of . . . treating me with the utmost kindness on account of a few alchemical secrets I taught him . . ." (Pierre Coste, *The Life and Works of Saint Vincent de Paul*, vol. 1, trans. Joseph Leonard, p. 35). It seems that he subsequently accompanied the vice-legate to Rome, but what happened there also remains a mystery. In any case, Vincent reappeared in France, deciding to try his fortune in Paris.

Toward the end of his life, Vincent sought to destroy the letters describing his legendary captivity written a half-century earlier. Indeed, modern biographers have discredited the particulars of Vincent's adventures. If nothing else, Vincent's exploits point to a time in his life when virtue took a distant place behind expediency.

For the most part, Vincent viewed his priesthood as a means of social advancement. In a letter to his mother after a few years in Paris, he alludes to the perils and hard knocks of his upward climb:

> I'm annoyed that I still have to stay around this city to again firm up my chances for advancement (which bad luck snatched away from me) and can't therefore come back home to you and help you in the way I should. But I have such hope in God's goodness that he will bless my hard work and soon give me the wherewithal for an honorable retirement and for spending the rest of my days with you. (*Documents*, vol. 1, p. 18)

Making His Way in Paris

In Paris, Vincent managed to be appointed as the alms distributor for the former queen, Marie de Valois. While working at her palace, he shared a room with a struggling lawyer. One day Vincent was sick at home and ordered medicine from a druggist. The delivery man brought the medicine but rifled the attorney's luggage as he left. When the lawyer came home and discovered the money gone, he accused Vincent. In his anger, the lawyer spread the word that the priest could not be trusted. This accusation placed a cloud over Vincent, who had to move into a poor section of the city.

Around this time, Vincent came under the influence of Pierre de Bérulle, a spiritual director, influential writer on the spiritual life, and leader of a reform movement in the French church. Later a cardinal and key figure in the intrigues between Rome and the French court, Bérulle had founded the

Oratory in Paris and introduced the Carmelite renewal into the country. While at times their relationship was stormy, Bérulle spotted substance and promise in the young priest who came to him for guidance. Vincent prized Bérulle's wisdom. Indeed, Bérulle's direction propelled Vincent into a new phase of his spiritual journey.

Bérulle arranged for Vincent to take charge of a parish in Clichy, a small village near Paris. Here, the young priest felt the first flush of success in ministry. The parishioners responded enthusiastically to his care. The parish thrived. In a letter to a bishop that he wrote later in life, Vincent reminisced:

> I had a parish where people were so good and so responsive in doing everything I told them that, when I suggested to them they go to confession the first Sunday of each month, no one stayed away. . . . I would see from day to day the effect it had on them. I was so pleased with this, so touched, that I used to say to myself: "My God, how blessed I am to have such good people!" And I used to add: "No one could be happier than I, not you, your excellency, not even his holiness, the Pope." (*Documents*, vol. 9, p. 646)

After a year at Clichy, Vincent acceded to Bérulle's advice again. Leaving a curate to look after the little parish, Vincent took the position of chaplain and tutor to the de Gondi family in Paris. Rich, powerful, at the center of French social, military, and even religious life, the de Gondis were a family to be reckoned with. In a short time, Vincent became an influential member of the household, especially with Frances-Margaret de Silly, Madame de Gondi. While in her service as confidante and adviser, Vincent discovered his life's work.

The Conversion Begins

Vincent's change of heart began in the middle of one of his visits to the tenants of the de Gondi estates. When Vincent was called to hear the confession of a dying man, the spiritual naïveté of the penitent shocked Vincent. The poor man knew next to nothing about his religion. After Vincent left, the dying man begged to see Madame de Gondi to express his thanks for being able to speak to such a holy man. Soon Madame de Gondi pressed Vincent to do something more to spread the Gospel. His immediate response was to preach a sermon on general confession in the village chapel of Folleville on 25 January 1617, the feast of Paul's conversion.

The sermon and its consequences opened Vincent's eyes. In it, he asked the people to take to heart the necessity of repentance. The response overwhelmed him. For hours the villagers stood in line to go to confession. Inside they poured out their longing for the Gospel and for good priests to minister to them. Vincent had not guessed at their hunger, their need.

In years to come, Vincent looked back to this sermon as the turning point in his spiritual journey. He came to see that God's hand was leading him to preach the Gospel to poor people. In fact, eight years later, Vincent founded his band of priests and brothers, the Congregation of the Mission, on the strength of this experience in Folleville. But other influences were also at work to change Vincent from a fortune-seeking cleric to a servant of God's poor.

The Galleys and Confraternity of Charity

Philip de Gondi served as General of the Galleys. As commander of the Mediterranean fleet, he felt responsible for the spiritual welfare of the prisoners condemned to row the French warships. He asked Vincent to minister to the galley slaves. With zest, Vincent took up the work. Within a year, he had not only organized a series of missions among the convicts, but had successfully lobbied for the construction of more humane prisons as well. In addition, he set up a relief organization for the prisoners and their families.

In the year before Vincent went to work among the convicts, he began to develop another organization that lasts to the present day. While temporarily serving in a parish at Chatillon-les-Dombes in southeast France, he noticed that the parishioners could be momentarily generous to neighbors in crisis, but their care tended to wane when a problem continued. So Vincent organized an assistance association, named the Confraternity of Charity, that was based in the parish and attended to the long-term needs of the sick and impoverished parishioners. Vincent provided guidelines for this Confraternity, and in a short time similar groups sprang up all over France. These Confraternities live on today in groups like the Ladies of Charity and, through Frederick Ozanam in the nineteenth century, the Vincent de Paul Society.

God was drawing Vincent one step at a time to the type of service and, more fundamentally, the kind of love for which he became famous. First, God called him to rural evangelization, then to minister to galley slaves and, eventually, to all poor people.

The Congregation of the Mission

Vincent's ministry in Clichy and Chatillon-des-Dombes convinced him that people in rural France had been virtually abandoned by the church. Ambitious priests, like Vincent had been, flocked to the cities for the rewards there. His patrons, the de Gondis, also saw the problem of the unchurched rural areas and worried about the religious welfare of the people who worked and lived on their extensive properties in the countryside.

Casting about for some way of ensuring ministry on the estates, Madame de Gondi turned to Vincent. In fact, Vincent had been thinking along similar lines. Madame de Gondi asked Vincent to organize and direct a community of missionaries to work in rural areas. She set aside a considerable sum of money to begin the community and bought a building in which to house the group.

Vincent gathered a little band of missionaries to his side. In 1626, Vincent and three priests pledged to "aggregate and associate to ourselves and to the aforesaid work to live together as a Congregation, . . . and to devote ourselves to the salvation of the aforesaid poor country folk" (Coste, *Life and Works*, vol. 1, p. 152).

The Congregation of the Mission was born. Soon the community received the letters patent from the French throne, and, within several more years, approbation of the pope. More men joined Vincent and his three original companions and began preaching all across France. Within Vincent's lifetime, the Congregation of the Mission had spread throughout the world.

Reform of the Clergy and Saint Lazare

For some years Vincent had been concerned about the need for reform of the French clergy. Then on a sweltering summer afternoon in 1628, Vincent was traveling in a coach with Bishop Augustin Potier of Beauvais. After lamenting about the sorry state of the clergy, they agreed that reform had to begin with the young men—before harmful habits took root. It suddenly occurred to the bishop to take the young men about to be ordained into his own household to give them a short course on the spiritual and liturgical elements of their ministry. He asked Vincent to organize this project.

Vincent drew up a program, and with priests from his Congregation gave the first workshop-retreat for the deacons of Beauvais. The bishop and deacons were delighted and inspired. The approach quickly proved so effective and popular that Vincent had trouble finding space for all the applicants.

Providentially, the prior of an aging monastery in Paris approached Vincent with a proposal that the Congregation take charge of the priory buildings and use them as a base for missions and retreats. Thus, in 1632, Vincent and his community came to Saint Lazare, a place whose name has been attached to the community ever since. In many places in the world, the members of his Congregation of the Mission are known as Lazarists.

The Congregation now had a home for the retreatants and for its members. Saint Lazare and its extensive property was already home to mentally ill people, lepers, errant sons of the nobility, priests in trouble, and many needy poor for whose care Vincent also assumed responsibility. In the wartime years ahead, it would serve as a major food and clothing distribution center. To the people of Paris, Saint Lazare became synonymous with help for anyone in need.

Vincent's concern for reform of the clergy did not end with the retreats. Eventually, his Congregation assumed direction of several French seminaries and offered regular continuing education programs for clergy.

Louise de Marillac and the Daughters of Charity

Besides organizing his congregation, preaching, and running retreats, Vincent also served as spiritual director for a growing number of people. One of these became important as a partner in Vincent's ministry and as a model for charity in action. Louise de Marillac had recently been widowed. Searching for a new focus and deeper meaning in her faith, she looked to Vincent. At the beginning of their relationship, Vincent concentrated on counseling Louise, but soon he saw her potential for leadership.

The Ladies of Charity, a coalition of noblewomen Vincent had organized to serve poor people, had grown and spread. Confraternities of Charity likewise had sprung up all over France. With all his commitments and foundations, Vincent found it impossible to oversee all of these charitable groups. And so he turned to Louise. The decision turned out to be blessed by providence. Despite frail health, Louise de Marillac traveled from town to town, visiting, guiding, and encouraging the fledgling organizations.

In due course, Vincent consented to assume direction of the Hôtel-Dieu, a large hospital in Paris, and to organize the Ladies of Charity to minister there. Social status was, however, a problem that hampered their work. Most of the Ladies of Charity came from the nobility, and French social custom frowned upon their doing the kind of menial tasks required in caring for sick people. The women improvised and sent their servants to perform most of the dirty work. Naturally, the servants grumbled about doing more than they already had to do and tended to take their frustrations out on the patients.

If care were to be given with consistency and love, Vincent and Louise realized that women from the humbler classes would have to give it. Fortunately, a number of younger women from rural areas began to appear at the charity foundations ready to assist. (The first was a poor village girl named Margaret Naseau.) These women lacked the education and social graces of the upper class, but because they came from the poorer classes, they were more willing to provide the necessary direct care.

Under Louise's direction, more young women joined what was becoming a community. In 1633, Louise welcomed several of them into her own home for training. They became the nucleus of the new congregation, the Daughters of Charity. In just a few months the community had quadrupled in membership. Louise and Vincent had started a new type of religious community. Years later, in a letter, Louise described to Vincent's secretary what he should tell young girls about the Daughters of Charity:

> You must make the young girls of Saint-Fergeau, who are asking to be accepted into the company of the Daughters of Charity, realise that this is not a religious order, even less a hospital from which they will never come out, but that the vocation calls for them to go looking for the sick poor in all sorts of places, no matter what the weather is like. (Luigi Mezzadri, *A Short Life of St. Vincent de Paul*, trans. Thomas Davitt, p. 63)

The Daughters of Charity were seculars, as Louise declared. They lived in houses, not convents; their cloister was the city streets; their enclosure was their commitment to God and service. They gave their lives to visiting the sick in their homes, ministering in hospitals, caring for prisoners, orphans, the mentally ill, and the homeless of Paris. They also taught catechism to rural children. The Daughters took no permanent vows, but annually recommitted themselves.

Louise was the prime organizer for the fledgling community, but Vincent, with his spirituality, his warm heart, and his great common sense, played an essential role in training the women. Out of their growing friendship and collaboration, Louise and Vincent had done something revolutionary—they had created a community of women who ministered outside the confines of a cloister. Eventually, apostolic congregations of women would multiply and flourish.

Vincent believed that all Christians had responsibility for announcing the Good News. His inclusion of women in the active apostolate was a logical outgrowth of this belief, even though it raised eyebrows and opposition at the time. Almost alone among his contemporaries, Vincent recognized the immense potential of women for spreading the Gospel. Vincent included them in most of his initiatives. He especially challenged wealthy women. For example, one of his most famous letters is a heartrending plea for these women to save orphans:

> Compassion and love led you to adopt these tiny creatures as your own children. Since . . . their mothers by nature deserted them, you became their mothers by grace. Just for a moment now, stop being their mothers and become their judges. You have the power of life or death over them right in your hands. Since the time is here to pass sentence, I'm going to take a vote to see whether or not you intend to show them clemency. If you continue your loving help for their sustenance, they will live. If you withdraw it, they will certainly pass away and die. Hard experience tells you there is no doubt about it. (*Documents*, vol. 13, p. 801)

Vincent did not stop at structuring new ways for women to contribute to the church's mission. He welcomed them as co-workers to evangelize poor people.

The Victims of War

In 1639, the area of Lorraine was devastated by war. Soldiers ravaged the farms and villages, stripping the territory bare. Vincent begged for help and, through the Ladies of Charity, collected money and other forms of aid. He sent members of his own Congregation to distribute the aid and to organize relief.

When the French provinces of Picardy and Champagne suffered devastation from the invading armies during the Thirty Years War, Vincent not only sent material help, but also sent Daughters of Charity to minister to the victims and refugees.

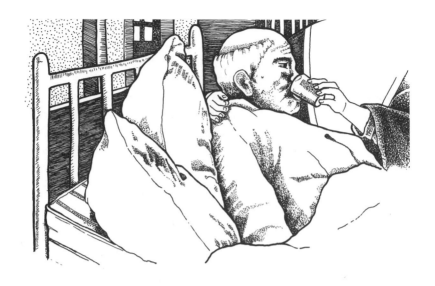

Finally, when a brutal civil war called the Fronde broke out in Paris and other parts of France, Vincent set up assistance programs and collected alms. He also tried to mediate peace by making a direct appeal to the queen to fire her minister of state, Cardinal Mazarin. When the queen refused, Vincent went directly to Mazarin and asked him to step down. These efforts not only failed, but caused Mazarin henceforth to turn a cold shoulder to Vincent and remove him from a high-level commission set up to guide the French church. As Vincent continued his peacemaking journey, his horse fell into an icy river. Although Vincent almost drowned, he recovered quickly and continued his exhausting trip. When he returned to Saint Lazare—looking forward to a much needed rest—he found the place teeming with hungry, dispossessed Parisians and refugees from various parts of France. Somehow, Vincent and his communities fed the hordes of people gathered at the gates and even managed to see God's providence in the middle of it all.

Jansenism

Part of the spiritual atmosphere of Vincent's day was a movement known as Jansenism. It arose from a rigorous interpretation of Saint Augustine's theology taught mainly by two champions, Cornelis Jansen and Jean de Hauranne, who was known more commonly as the Abbe of Saint Cyran.

Vincent had been on good terms with Saint Cyran and even defended his character when called upon by the Prime Minister, Cardinal Richelieu. But in subsequent years, the doctrinal and ascetic implications of Saint Cyran's teaching put great strain on their friendship. In 1641, matters between the two came to a head. Vincent took a strong position against the Jansenists as part of his role on the Council of Conscience. This high-level committee advised the French court about moral and religious issues.

From this time on, Vincent publicly opposed Jansenism, encouraged theologians who were writing against them, and even called a group of bishops together at Saint Lazare to put a stop to the debates fomented by Jansenism.

Vincent's primary objections to Jansenism were pastoral. Saint Cyran took an elitist view of the Gospels. He held that Jesus did not die for all men and women and held impossibly high standards for entering heaven. From Saint Cyran's point of view, few—if any—of Vincent's poor people could qualify as real Christians. Even though Vincent's opposition to Jansenism cost a number of wealthy backers for his projects, his conviction that Jansenism was spiritual poison remained firm.

Going out to the Whole World

By 1643, the Congregation of the Mission had established a house in Rome. Soon after, Vincent sent members of his community to Genoa, Turin, and Perugia. At a request from the Vatican, priests were dispatched to minister in Ireland. Other missionaries left for Scotland. When Queen Louise-Marie de Gonzague of Poland, a former Lady of Charity, asked Vincent to send members of the community, he once again agreed. This time Daughters of Charity accompanied the priests and set up their first foundation outside of France. By the end of Vincent's life, the Congregation of the Mission could be found in Tunis, Algiers, and Madagascar too.

Vincent's Final Days

Vincent carried on his work well into his seventies. With members of his foundations spread throughout France and the world, Vincent's correspondence was immense. During his lifetime he wrote more than thirty thousand letters. A constant stream of visitors came to Saint Lazare to seek his counsel. His growing infirmity forced Vincent to use a carriage to visit orphanages and other sites of his work, even though this apparent "luxury" embarrassed him.

In March of 1660, Louise de Marillac, his dear friend and generous collaborator, died. In the few months that he had left, Vincent's own health steadily declined. For many years, he had suffered from fevers and had recently developed painful ulcers on his legs. Nevertheless, he continued his voluminous correspondence and even gave a few conferences. By September 1660, Vincent knew that death was near. On September 26, he attended Mass and received Communion for the last time. Early morning of the next day, Vincent passed away. He was eighty years of age.

All of France mourned Vincent's death. At his funeral, the preacher declared that Vincent had transformed the face of the French church. No one disputed this claim. Funny, charming, impassioned, candid—Vincent had an extraordinary capacity to connect with all types of people and to get them to serve their needy neighbors. During his life, he saw to it that thousands of hungry people were fed, prisoners visited, clergy trained, naked clothed, sick nursed, orphans cared for. His basic vision was simply that the Good News should be announced to poor people. In his work, Vincent lived that vision.

Praying with Vincent de Paul

In the very practical choices that he made in his life, Vincent moved out toward his brothers and sisters and inward toward his God. His integrated spirituality cannot be described neatly, but some traits can be distinguished.

Follower of Christ, Evangelizer of the Poor

Jesus captivated Vincent. He set his course by what Jesus would do in any given circumstance. Vincent especially identified with the scene in Nazareth's synagogue, in which Jesus declared that his life's mission was to bring good news to the poor. In his conferences and letters, Vincent often reminded his followers of how fortunate they were to be doing exactly what Jesus Christ himself had come to do.

Vincent nurtured his love for God through prayer, but his ministry in turn informed and nourished his prayer. In his view, prayer and action walked hand in hand.

Love of God and Trust in God's Care

Vincent's strong love for his mother particularly disposed him to recognize the richness of Jesus' claim that his Father in heaven was lovable and gracious. Vincent's appreciation of God's parental care made him an attractive and believable evangelizer himself. One of his fundamental accomplishments was communicating God's love to the poor people of his day.

In turn, Vincent trusted this loving God. He urged his followers to draw closer in the same trust, to be sure that the work that they did really *was* God's work.

Warmhearted and Practical Love for the Poor

Vincent showed special concern for neglected people. They served as his window to God's activity in the world. They were "holy ground." In countless ways, Vincent taught that Jesus lived among the poor and outcast people. Vincent's love also took practical forms. He often emphasized that love needed to be shown in *a*ffect and *e*ffect.

Vincent had a special gift for drawing people into gospel service and then organizing them to work for the long-term good. Jesus' mission belonged to all Christians, and Vincent helped people become part of that mission.

Habits and Discipline

Vincent had little patience with hollow enthusiasm. The love he preached had to be put into concrete practice. Vincent insisted that those who would minister and evangelize must first develop the proper habits for their work. If Vincent's apostles were to serve effectively, they must possess certain abilities and strengths of character. Poor people, already suspicious and marginalized, would not trust anyone who was dishonest. The performance of Jesus' mission required character, hard work, empathy, listening, and detachment.

Vincent de Paul for Today

Many years after Vincent's death, during one popular uprising, rioting mobs broke into the Pantheon in Paris and smashed all the religious statues but one. Despite their zeal to overthrow what they perceived to be oppressive Christianity, they could not bring themselves to deface the image of Monsieur Vincent. He had done too much good, helped too many of their ancestors, spoken too movingly about the preciousness of the ordinary person for them to throw him out with the rest.

Praying with Vincent reminds us that serving our neighbor is serving God. Vincent models the fullness of a Christian life that is prayerfully active and actively prayerful.

God, Our Loving Parent

Theme: Vincent knew himself to be sustained by God's motherly and fatherly love.

Opening prayer: Strong and tender God, help me to sense your care as you hold me in the palm of your hand.

About Vincent

The religious seas of France raged during the later years of Vincent's life. The spiritual movement known as Jansenism formed the eye of the storm. Jansenism polarized people at the centers of political and ecclesiastical power. Since Vincent had by that time become nationally involved in church reform, he could not stay uninvolved in this issue. At one especially troublesome point, he testified in court on behalf of an old ally, the Abbot of Saint Cyran, a Jansenist leader who was under attack from Cardinal Richelieu's government. Vincent resisted sacrificing a friend for the sake of the cardinal's political agenda.

However, some years later, Vincent began to take strong issue with the Jansenists' spirituality. The abbot's writings had taken on an increasingly fearful edge. Vincent's friend now preached about a forbiddingly cold, judgmental God who looked harshly at sinful human beings. Jansenists like the abbot held that human nature was corrupted at its core by original sin.

Vincent could not conceive of such a harsh and dreadful God. From his boyhood, he had prayed to the all-merciful, warm, and loving Father of Jesus, an Abba who called all of his children beloved. Vincent rested and warmed himself in God's parental care and protection.

Vincent could make some allowances for the rough-and-tumble of Jansenist politics, but he could not abide their sense of the Divine. He could not imagine loading the yoke of such an intimidating God onto the shoulders of the suffering poor people of France. Compassion, in Vincent's view, was God's name.

Vincent denied the Jansenist views not only in public but also while giving spiritual direction. When one of Vincent's correspondents was suffering through a difficult period after the death of both parents, Vincent wrote these words back to him:

> Surely, the great secret of the spiritual life is to abandon all we love to him by abandoning ourselves to all God wishes in perfect confidence that all will be for the best. . . . He will take the place of father and mother for you. He will be your consolation, your virtue, and in the end the recompense of your love. (*Documents*, vol. 8, pp. 255–256)

In strong contrast to the growing Jansenist view of God, Vincent's God was Abba—a loving parent.

Pause: Ponder this question: In my prayer, do I sense myself being taken into the arms and onto the lap of a loving, parental God?

Vincent's Words

In a conversation just a few months before his death, Vincent disclosed what it was that had most nourished him. He said:

> To be consumed for God, to have no goods nor power except for the purpose of expending them for God. That is what Our Savior did himself, he who was consumed for love of his Father. (*Documents*, vol. 13, p. 179)

In another instance, Louise de Marillac became distressed that she was not doing God's will because she could not accomplish all of the resolutions that she had made. Vincent offered this simple reminder:

> Do not worry yourself when you fail to carry them out. God is love and wishes us to go to Him by love. So do not look upon yourself as being obliged to carry out all these good resolutions. (Coste, *Life and Works*, vol. 3, p. 365)

Reflection

Vincent's amazing accomplishments required that he maintain a prodigious pace. Nevertheless, contemporaries marveled at his calm and confidence. Even working closely with desperately poor or sick people, in the midst of chaotic surroundings, Vincent lived with surehanded peacefulness.

When Vincent read the Gospels, he took great comfort from the relationship between Jesus and Abba. Jesus the Son can heal and forgive because he basks in the loving gaze of God, his loving parent. To be truly good and whole, every human action should model itself on the circle of loving communion between Jesus and his Abba. Vincent learned this lesson well.

He also learned of God's constant love from the poor people with whom he worked. In small and large ways, they embodied God's motherly and fatherly love. Vincent knew that he could rely on God's care when he took on "impossible" tasks or when his own light failed him. Faith in God's inexhaustible tenderness nourished Vincent's resiliency.

✧ Reflect on your own predominant images of God with these questions for guides:
✦ When you pray, what image of God most often comes to mind?
✦ Do you feel that you have to select the right words or avoid certain topics in your conversations with God?
✦ Do you sometimes find yourself praying to a harsh or dispassionate God? If so, recall one particular instance and reflect on why you imagined God this way.

✦ Have you found yourself praying to God, the loving parent? If so, what were the circumstances of this experience? How did you feel during this prayer time?

✧ To refresh your image of God as loving parent, you might read and reflect on these passages from the Scriptures: Psalms 23:1; 121:5; Isaiah 40:10–11; Matthew 6:8–15; 11:25–27; Luke 11:13; John 1:1; 1 John 4:8.

✧ Pray these words of Vincent slowly and repeatedly, pondering their meaning for you: God will be my "consolation, . . . virtue, . . . the recompense of . . . love."

✧ Bring to mind a situation in which presently you feel out of control, in chaos. Who is there? What is happening? How do you feel? Then imagine that God is with you at your side. Ask God for the grace you need to cope with this situation. What does God tell you about the situation? Listen. Then repeat silently this prayer from Psalm 62: You, God, are "my rock, my safety, my stronghold so that I stand unshaken."

✧ Recall a time when the sense of God's presence helped you stand calm and secure in the midst of chaos and suffering. In your mind's eye, put yourself back into the scene. How did you sense God's support? How did you feel? Was there a person there who radiated confidence and provided support and affirmation? Give thanks to God for the serenity and strength God gave you.

✧ In this guided meditation, you are invited to encounter Jesus:

> Close your eyes. . . . Relax. . . . Let all the tension go. . . . Breathe deeply in and out . . . in and out. . . . Feel the tensions leave your feet. . . . If you need to, tense your muscles and then just let them relax . . . now your legs. . . . Relax your stomach and chest. . . . Now let all the tensions escape from your arms . . . your neck. . . . Let your jaw and face relax, too. . . . Slow

down . . . hear the breath of life flowing calmly in and out. . . .

Now see yourself on a hill overlooking Jerusalem. . . . Jesus and his disciples are walking by. . . . At the crest of the hill, Jesus stops and gazes down at the city. . . . Pain creases his face. . . . You overhear his whispered words: "Jerusalem, Jerusalem. How I have longed to gather you into my arms as a mother hen gathers her young under her wings."

. . . He notices you standing there with him. . . . Holding out his arms to you, you walk to him, and he embraces you. . . . Gathered into his embrace, you tell him what is in your heart. . . .

When you have finished, you separate. Jesus looks into your eyes. . . . Then he continues his journey into Jerusalem. . . . You watch him walking down the hill. . . .

When you are ready, return from the scene and open your eyes.

After this guided meditation, you might wish to write any reactions in your journal.

✧ Imagine that John the Baptist has just poured the Jordan's warm water over you. Repeat these words, adapted from the Scriptures, as a prayer of divine affirmation: "I am God's beloved child." Stand on the bank of the river; let the meaning of the words seep into you.

✧ This prayer hangs over the kitchen sink of a harried mother of four children. In a busy time, pray it with her:

The air
    the mothering air, the hollows,
        nest of birds,
    these things remind me always
        of a God who holds us in herself
            as in a womb.
        (John Shea, *The God Who Fell from Heaven*, p. 7)

God's Word

Can a woman forget her baby at the breast,
feel no pity for the child she has borne?
Even if these were to forget,
I shall not forget you.
Look, I have engraved you on the palms of my hands.

(Isaiah 49:15–16)

Closing prayer: All-loving God, surround me with your mercy and love. Let me feel the firmness of your hand, especially when I feel blown in a thousand directions. Let me know the depths of your care for me and for all of your people.

✧ **Meditation 2** ✧

Following God's Will

Theme: Vincent prayed that over time his designs and actions would be more and more in harmony with God's desires. He knew that this was the way to a full life.

Opening prayer: All-provident God, I put all of my thoughts and impulses, my biases and viewpoints, my action and waiting, my plans and confusion into your hands. Lead me on your way.

About Vincent

One afternoon in the very last months of his life, Vincent sat with some of his close friends. In the way that people sometimes do when they sense that their time is coming to an end, Vincent began to speak about what mattered to him most. He did not tell of any particularly successful project, or of people whom he had loved and who had loved him, nor even of his precious poor ones. Rather, he talked to his friends about the loving hand of God that had led him, of the interior star that had steered him through all the hectic years. Bent and elderly as he was, he declared, "We should give ourselves to God and wear ourselves out for God" (*Documents*, vol. 11, p. 402).

Everything, he said, revolved around doing what God had in mind. Warming to his subject, he continued: "And I myself, old and infirm as I am, should not stop being open to God, yes, even to set out for the Indies to win souls for Christ even if I should die on the way or aboard ship" (*Documents*, vol. 11, p. 402).

His hearers could hardly be surprised by his words. Following the will of God had been Vincent's way for as long as they could remember. A few of the older ones could still recall the steamy summer day almost fifty years before when young Monsieur Vincent led them on a special pilgrimage up the side of Montmartre in Paris. When they reached the shrine on top, he had them all kneel down. Then, in their name, he prayed, "for the grace of not having anything other than God and of doing everything for God" (Mezzadri, *Short Life*, p. 29). And for all the years since that day in Montmartre, Vincent's beacon, his interior compass had been that same gracious will.

Pause: Ask yourself: In the decisions that I have made during the last few days, have I stopped to ask what God willed for me to do?

Vincent's Words

In the only systematic work that Vincent wrote, a rule of life for priests, he gave this advice:

> A sure way for a Christian to grow rapidly in holiness is a conscientious effort to carry out God's will in all circumstances. . . . Each one should show a great eagerness in that sort of openness to God's will which Christ and the saints developed so carefully. This means that we should not have a disproportionate liking for any ministry, person or place, especially our native land, or for anything of that sort. We should even be ready and willing to leave all these gladly. (*Constitutions*, pp. 108, 112)

A decade earlier, trying to encourage a confused missionary to find the true bearings in his life, Vincent wrote:

So, father, let us ask Our Lord that everything might be done according to his providence, that our wills be submitted to him in such a way that between him and us there might be only one, which will enable us to enjoy his unique love in time and eternity. (*Documents*, vol. 2, p. 469)

Reflection

A spirituality that rarely translates into action can certainly be questioned. On the other hand, undiscerned activity can simply be a person's compulsions at work.

Vincent took on one complicated project after another and at times exhausted himself in the process. However, he always discerned each initiative carefully to be sure that it was rooted in God's will. He could never be accused of activity for its own sake.

Vincent studied the Gospels, asked for advice, and prayed for God's light and strength. Then he acted—confidently—trusting that he had done his best to give flesh to God's intent.

✧ Think back to an occasion when the sense of God working within you was especially strong? Who was involved? What were you doing? How did you feel? Converse with God about this time when you walked together.

✧ Slowly, pausing after each recitation, pray these words of Jesus repeatedly: "My food is to do the will and complete the work of the one who sent me" (adapted from John 4:34).

✧ When he was an old man, Vincent declared that he was open to doing God's will even if it meant setting out for the Indies and dying on board the ship. Being open to God's will may mean sacrificing some treasured beliefs or possessions. Complete Vincent's phrase in your own way. Try out different things that you might find hard to abandon if you should discern that God's will was leading you in a new direction:

"I myself, just as I am, should not stop being open to God, yes, even if I should. . . ."

Pray for the graces you need to say yes to God's promptings, no matter what.

✧ Most of the time, recognizing God's will is easier after the fact. But living the Christian life requires that we make decisions, that we follow God's will. List several decisions facing you. Then pick one to pray with.

✦ First, pray for God's help, using this prayer adapted from Saint Paul's words to the Ephesians (1:3,8–9): Blessed be you, my God. In all wisdom and comprehension, you make your will known to us through Jesus, your son. Make your will known to me so that I might live and act as Jesus did.

✦ Peruse the Gospels for passages that might throw God's light on your decision. Trust the Holy Spirit to lead you. Meditate on what the Scriptures reveal to you.

✦ If you have a wise friend, share your questions and thinking with him or her. Ask for help in making your choices.

✦ Lay your decisions before God. Ask for the Holy Spirit's light to see God's will and also for the courage to act accordingly.

✧ Thomas Merton, one of the greatest spiritual writers of the twentieth century, talked about acting from our "false center" or our "true center." Our false center consists of superficial wants and ill-considered, often falsely elevated expectations. Our true center is the inmost spot within us where God dwells and speaks. Acting from our false center most frequently leads to uneasiness, disharmony, and incompleteness. Acting from our true center brings comprehension, affirmation, and fullness. Reflect back. Try to name times when you acted out of your false self. Why did you do so? What were the effects? Then try to specify instances when you knew that God's will grounded your actions. How did you feel? What were the results? Talk with God about how you become caught in the false center and about the grace you need to act out of your true center more consistently.

✧ Slowly read the story of the Annunciation (Luke 1:26-36). When you have read it one or more times, close your eyes. In your imagination, put yourself in the room, watching Mary agree to become the mother of the Emmanuel, God-with-us. What does she look like? How does she react? Hear her say, "You see before you [God's] servant, let it happen to me as you have said."

Now picture some difficult situations in which you find yourself with people you find hard to deal with. Knowing that God's will calls you to a life of charity, pray Mary's words about each situation or person: "You see before you [God's] servant."

God's Word

I am the bread of life. Hunger will be unknown to those who come to me. No one who believes in me will suffer thirst. I would never abandon anyone who follows me. After all, I became flesh and blood to do the will of the one who sent me, not to do my own will. It is the divine will that whoever believes in the Son shall have life eternal. I tell you, believers will be raised up on the last day.

(Adapted from John 6:35–40)

Closing prayer: "Grant me the grace, [loving God] . . . to begin as of this very moment to live in the bliss of the saints in heaven, which consists in being one, in willing and not-willing, with God's [own] self" (*Documents*, vol. 10, pp. 285–286).

Jesus Christ, the Center

Theme: For Vincent, true holiness meant that all of his decisions, plans, struggles, and actions had to revolve around the person of Jesus Christ.

Opening prayer: Jesus, be my light and my life. Let my eyes be like the servant's eyes, always looking to do your bidding.

About Vincent

One day, in an expansive mood, Vincent opened his soul to some of his friends. He felt blessed and extremely fortunate because he was doing what Jesus had done. He told his companions:

> To make God known to the poor, to tell them that the Kingdom of Heaven is at hand and that it is for the poor— O how great that is, so sublime is it to preach the gospel to the poor that is above all the office of the Son of God. (*Documents*, vol. 12, p. 80)

His own relationship with Jesus Christ developed in three stages. During his boyhood, his parents passed on their convictions about Jesus. Vincent believed, but not enough to move mountains. The second stage occurred in his twenties. A string of personal defeats and some sound spiritual direction caused Vincent to look deeply into himself. In ways known only to Vincent and God, Vincent's encounter with Jesus moved him to rearrange the map of his life.

Finally, as he became more involved in ministering to rural people and the poor of Paris, Vincent discovered Jesus Christ in the faces of these humble souls. More and more, Vincent's life revolved around the person of Jesus, whom he encountered in poor, sick, and homeless people. Upon reading the rule to the Daughters of Charity after it had been approved, he told them:

> The Confraternity of Charity of the servants of the parochial sick poor. . . . O Mon Dieu! What a lovely title and what a beautiful description! . . . *Servants of the poor,* that is just the same as to say *Servants of Jesus Christ,* for He regards as done to Himself what is done to them, and they are His members. And what did He do whilst on earth but serve the poor? (Coste, *Life and Works,* vol. 1, p. 355)

He saw Christ in poor people, but he also found Jesus the source of his unity with others. Mademoiselle du Fay, a devoted and generous benefactor to Vincent's work, also came to Vincent for spiritual direction. Whenever Vincent had to go on a journey, he would inform Mademoiselle du Fay. In one note to her, he said:

> I did not let you know I was going. Will you please forgive me? Will you not let me know, pray, how your dear heart has taken this? . . . Well now, I trust [our hearts] will be in complete harmony in the Heart that contains them both, and that is the Heart of Our Lord. . . . Always be gay, Mademoiselle, I beseech you and, to that end, honour Our Lord's holy tranquillity of soul, and be fully confident that He will guide your holy heart by the holy love of His own. (Coste, *Life and Works,* vol. 1, p. 299)

To Vincent, Jesus simply was love, the source of Vincent's strength, vision, and harmony.

Pause: Ponder this question: How much of a compass is the person of Jesus for orienting my choices in life?

Vincent's Words

Trying to encourage one of his early collaborators, Vincent wrote:

> Remember, Father, that we live in Jesus Christ by the death of Jesus Christ and that we ought to die in Jesus Christ by the life of Jesus Christ and that our life ought to be hidden in Jesus Christ and full of Jesus Christ and that in order to die like Jesus Christ it is necessary to live like Jesus Christ. (*Documents,* vol. 1, p. 295)

In wonder at Jesus' love for his people, Vincent prayed:

> O Savior! How happy were those who had the good fortune to approach you! What a countenance! What meekness, what openness of manner you showed in order to attract them! With what confidence you inspired people to approach you! O, what signs of love! (*Documents,* vol. 12, p. 190)

Reflection

Jesus' words and, perhaps more so, his actions inspired Vincent. The dynamic, vigorous Jesus moved Vincent to free prisoners, console sick people, and radiate hope to poor souls. Vincent believed and experienced the truth of Jesus' claim that his food and drink was in the doing of his Abba's will.

Vincent sent his own followers out into the whole world to build the Reign of God. Vincent himself lived like the Hassidic teacher who packed his bags whenever he went to pray, just in case God asked him on the spot to go somewhere and do something. Any missionary whose heart resided with Jesus had to be ready to move, to act in Jesus' name.

✧ Meditatively read "Vincent's Words" again. Spend time listening to Vincent speak these words to you. When you come across a passage that is especially enlightening or perplexing, talk about the passage with Vincent. Ask him what the passage means. Talk about why you find it illuminating or challenging. When you have concluded your dialog, write down some of your reflections about "Vincent's Words."

✧ Go back to a time when some special person gradually became "enshrined" inside you. How did the relationship begin? How did you deepen the relationship? What habits-of-the-heart did you form between you? Then, reflect on this question: Are there parallels between the development of my relationship with this special person and the story of my relationship with Jesus?

✧ In Vincent's day, the notion of "Rule" meant a definition of a lifestyle, an aggregate of the attitudes, habits, and behaviors intended to permeate everyday existence. Vincent encouraged his listeners to take Jesus Christ as the Rule for their life. Write a list of three values or "rules" of life that would be central to Jesus Christ. Dialog with Jesus about the ways in which you can best follow this Rule.

✧ The apostle "Doubting" Thomas accepted Jesus as his Savior by demanding proof. Imagine yourself sitting next to Thomas. What questions about Jesus frequently nag you? What doubts weaken your faith? Jesus is with you. Ask him your questions. Engage him in conversation about your doubts, fears, and shaky beliefs. Then slowly and repeatedly pray Thomas' words, "My Lord and my God."

✧ Especially in eastern Christianity, the "Jesus Prayer" has helped believers center themselves on Christ. Do some deep breathing, focusing your attention on the air as it is drawn into your lungs and then is released. Breathe deeply and slowly, concentrating on the breath. When you are relaxed, pray the words, "Jesus, Servant of God," when you inhale, and "Send me to do God's work" on your exhale. Continue this prayer for your entire prayer period.

God's Word

But what were once my assets I now through Christ Jesus count as losses. Yes, I will go further: because of the supreme advantage of knowing Christ Jesus. (Philippians 3:7–8)

Closing prayer: O God, grant that we may walk in your steps. Send the grace to follow your example. Lead us to seek the reign of God and its justice, and to leave all other worries in your care (*Documents*, vol. 12, pp. 147–148).

✧ **Meditation 4** ✧

God's Loving Direction in Our Life

Theme: Convinced that he was held in the palm of God's hand, Vincent let himself be led by that same gracious hand.

Opening prayer: Provident, loving God, protect and defend me in my weakness and guide me with your light.

About Vincent

When he was nearly seventy years old, Vincent limped back into Paris—after a bone-numbing relief tour of a war zone in winter—and faced the immediate crisis of feeding the thousands of emaciated refugees camped at his front door. He had turned his headquarters into a great relief center but, for all the efforts of many generous people, the center had come to the end of its resources.

At the end of Vincent's first hectic day back, the treasurer timidly broke the news to Vincent that nothing remained in the bank. Vincent looked up into the tired eyes of his companion and replied: "That's good news. Now we can show we trust God" (Mezzadri, *Short Life*, p. 56). Within the week, new money came.

For Vincent, providence meant trusting in God's care, but also allowing providence to give direction, sometimes down paths that appeared most unpromising. Early on, for example, Vincent felt drawn toward the missions. He had sent out a sizable number of men and women to evangelize overseas. The missionary work in Madagascar, however, had exacted a high price: Everyone that Vincent had sent to Madagascar had died there or on the journey there. To say the least, members of the Congregation were having serious second thoughts about working in Madagascar.

For Vincent, the matter had been settled. In a pointed letter, he explained:

> Some members of the Company may say perhaps that Madagascar should be abandoned; flesh and blood will speak that language and say that no more men should be sent there. But I am certain that the Spirit says otherwise. . . . It would be quite some Company, that of the Mission, if because five or six had died, it were to abandon the work of the Lord. (*Documents*, vol. 11, p. 420)

Pause: Ask yourself: What have I actually done with the inner promptings to do something beautiful for God?

Vincent's Words

> We ought to have confidence in God that he will look after us since we know for certain that as long as we are grounded in that sort of love and trust we will be always under the protection of God in heaven, we will remain unaffected by evil and never lack what we need even when everything we possess seems headed for disaster. (*Constitutions*, p. 108)

> Do not worry yourself overmuch. . . . Grace has its moments. Let us abandon ourselves to the providence of God and be very careful not to run ahead of it. If it pleases God to give us some consolation in our calling, it is this: that . . . we have tried to follow his great providence in everything. (*Documents*, vol. 2, p. 453)

But what are we going to do, you say? We will do what Our Lord wills which is to keep ourselves always in dependence on his Providence. (*Documents*, vol. 2, p. 469)

Reflection

As a culture, we do not feel confident in our ability to read an overall purpose into life's events. Life often seems perilous at best. Things seem to "just happen," and we try to adjust as best we can. In such a constantly startling world, how do we maintain trust in a God who is said to care for us and guide us?

Because Vincent served the most vulnerable people in French society, he knew precariousness firsthand. But he had also developed the habit of reading God's hand by hindsight. He looked back at seemingly chance events and discerned patterns of God's solicitude at work. For instance, when asked how his many works began, Vincent pointed to a particular sermon that he had given to an audience of poor land-tenants. Even though he recognized that the sermon was effective at the time, only later did he understand its success as God's way of telling him that ministry ought to be his life's direction. Such recognition did not come automatically. Vincent had consciously developed the practice of reflecting on those things that seemed to "just happen" to look for God's finger in them. Past events were mine shafts laced with veins of God's call and God's care.

Vincent's growing faith in God's providence, as he viewed it in hindsight, gave him the confidence he needed to reach out even more boldly to poor and oppressed people. Indeed, he knew that God's providence was available to all Christians and could be their sustenance.

✧ Vincent said: "Grace has its moments. Let us abandon ourselves to the providence of God and be very careful not to run ahead of it." Recall several key turning points in your life's journey, points along the way when, unknown to you at the time, your life was being changed. In writing, describe the images that come to mind when you remember these turning points when grace "had its moment." Then try to name specific ways in which the guiding hand of God was leading you to truth and a fuller life. Praise and thank God for such grace.

✧ Slowly and prayerfully, savor the words of this famous hymn by John Henry Newman, "The Pillar of the Cloud," that celebrates God's guiding care:

> Lead, kindly Light, amid the encircling gloom,
>   Lead Thou me on!
> The night is dark, and I am far from home—
>   Lead Thou me on!
> Keep Thou my feet; I do not ask to see
> The distant scene—one step enough for me.
>
> I was not ever thus, nor prayed that Thou
>   Shouldst lead me on.
> I loved to choose and see my path; but now
>   Lead Thou me on!
> I loved the garish day, and, spite of fears,
> Pride ruled my will: remember not past years.
>
> So long Thy power hath blessed me, sure it still
>   Will lead me on,
> O'er moor and fen, o'er crag and torrent, till
>   The night is gone;
> And with the morn those Angel faces smile
> Which I have loved long since, and lost awhile.

✧ Bring to mind a decision facing you right now, especially a decision that perhaps you have been delaying and worrying about for a long time. Write a letter to Vincent, outlining all of your fears and confusion, hopes, and reasons.

Imagine then that after a month, you find Vincent's response in your mailbox. (Recall that during his life, he wrote over thirty thousand letters!) You open the letter and read:

> My God, [your name], what great hidden treasures there are in holy Providence. How marvelously Our Lord is honored by those who follow it and do not kick against it. (*Documents*, vol. 1, p. 68)

You decide to consider your decision in light of his words. What "hidden treasures" reside in the decision you need to make? How is God's Reign best integrated into this decision? Are you "kicking" against a course of action that would be more life giving? Like night vision given by the headlights of a car, our understanding cannot be stretched until we actually begin to move. Decide what concrete steps you need to take to move on your decision. Pray for the guidance of the Holy Spirit; talk with God about your decision.

✧ In your mind's eye, take yourself back to an environment in which you felt entirely safe. It could be anywhere. Maybe as a child you loved burrowing under the cushions of your living room couch, or maybe you crawled into your tree house or into a parent's lap. Perhaps the safe shelter is in the embrace of a loved one. Imagine that you are in that place now. Breathe deeply. Relax. When you feel safe and secure, speak with God about some issue that has been unsettling or threatening you. Lay it out before God. Then hold it out to God and try to hand it over. Remind yourself that this safe haven is only a shadow of God's shelter. Finally, ask God what you should do next.

✧ Pray slowly and repeatedly: "Do not worry yourself overmuch. The rest will come in its time." As you pray, offer to God each worry that is bothering you.

God's Word

If God is for us, why worry about anyone who opposes us? After all, if God sent Jesus the Savior, God's very son, for our sake, won't God give us anything else we need? . . . God loves us. So I am convinced that nothing, not death, or life, or angels, or governments, or anything else in all of creation can separate us from the love of God that we have been given in Jesus Christ.

(Adapted from Romans 8:31–32,37–39)

Closing prayer:

O my God,
  I want to give myself to you,
  body and soul, heart and mind and spirit,
  for the realizations of your designs for my life.
  (Frits Braakhuis, *Praying in St. Vincent's Spirit*, no. 17)

✧ Meditation 5 ✧

Evangelization

Theme: Vincent accepted the call from Jesus to go out in the world to preach and teach the Good News. Evangelization stood at the core of Vincent's spirituality.

Opening prayer: O God who rescues and saves, draw me more closely into the circle of your life. Strengthen me, energize me, and sensitize me so that I may be the compassionate hands and passionate voice of Jesus in my world.

About Vincent

When Vincent first came to Paris as a young man, he clearly intended to make a name and a fortune for himself. He maneuvered to make the right connections and shrewdly kept his eye out for any possible advancement. Eventually, Vincent found his way into the good graces of Queen Marie, widow of King Henry IV. Soon he kept company with members of her palatial household. Nevertheless, two events turned Vincent away from fortune hunting and toward the mission of Jesus.

First, Vincent came under the powerful influence of Pierre de Bérulle, the famous spiritual director and writer. Bérulle kept emphasizing that Jesus is the incarnate Word of God who was *sent* to bear God's goodness and holiness to all of humankind. Gradually Vincent felt God's great energy sending him as well, although he still was not sure to whom.

Not long after Vincent came under Bérulle's direction, he began visiting a local welfare hospital. He brought Communion to the destitute people there, heard their confessions, and spoke with the poorest of Paris' many poor people. Slowly a light flickered on: Might these be the people to whom he was being sent?

In 1611, the Master of the Paris Mint gave fifteen thousand livres—a considerable sum of money—to Vincent as a personal gift. The next day, Vincent handed the whole sum over to the Brothers at the hospital. Now Vincent realized to whom God was directing him.

Later, in a conference, Vincent told his listeners about his own sense of mission and about the evangelizing mission of all Christians:

> To make God known to the poor; to announce Jesus Christ to them; to tell them that the Kingdom of Heaven is at hand! But that we should be called to associate with, and to share in, the works of the Son of God surpasses our understanding. What! To render ourselves—I do not dare say it—so great, so sublime, it is to preach the gospel to the poor, for it is above all else the office of the Son of God, and we are applied to it as instruments by which the Son of God continues to do from heaven what he once did on earth. Great reason have we . . . to praise God and to thank him unceasingly for this grace! (*Documents*, vol. 12, p. 80)

Preaching "the gospel to the poor" became the passion of Vincent's life. He never questioned again what he was sent to do and to whom he was sent.

Pause: Reflect on what part evangelizing has in your response to Jesus.

Vincent's Words

In another presentation, Vincent's passion focused more closely on evangelism's capacity to simultaneously draw the evangelizer nearer to both Christ and to Christ's people:

In our calling, we are patterned more closely on Our Lord Jesus Christ, who, it would seem, made it his principal task to assist and care for the poor: "He sent me to preach the Good News to the poor." And if somebody asked Our Lord, "Why did you come on earth?" (he would answer): "To assist the poor." "For any other reason?" "To assist the poor . . ." And so, are we not then the happiest of people to be part of the Mission for the very same reason that moved God to become one of us? (*Documents*, vol. 11, p. 108)

Reflection

Those who knew Vincent de Paul in his twenties would have had difficulty recognizing him in his forties. Something profound had happened. He was marching vigorously to a different drummer. Through his prayer, his discernment with a wise spiritual director, and his direct service with poor people, Vincent encountered Jesus and discovered his own and the Christian vocation: to preach the Gospel, especially to poor people.

God blesses all people with a zone of illumination in the middle of which they most clearly see God's face. This "God spot" might be in the electricity of an intimate relationship, in the awe evoked by nature's beauty, or in the subtle excitement of sharing insights while teaching or counseling. Jesus assures his disciples that bringing the Good News to other people is a "God spot." God is encountered in the very act of sharing the Gospel. While evangelizing, God sends the energy and power of grace. In giving, the evangelizer is evangelized.

✧ Read the section "Vincent's Words" again slowly and meditatively. Imagine that these words are directed to you. Ponder these questions:

✦ How do I feel about Vincent's directions?
✦ What prejudices, possessions, or relationships will I have to let go of?
✦ To what poor people am I being sent?

✧ Who are the people who draw you to God? What people are "God spots" for you? Bring their faces to mind. Hear their voices. They are your Spirit-bearers. Offer prayers of gratitude to God for them. If you have lost touch with any one of them, write, call, or visit this Spirit-bearer.

✧ Write your impressions of an instant in your life when you felt that you were praying as you acted, a time when you felt God's presence more in the doing of something than in contemplating it afterward.

✧ Visit a sick or shut-in person. Clean the house of someone who is unable to do so. Mind the children of someone who needs a short break. In other words, spread the Gospel by being the Good News to someone today.

✧ List five ways that you can "make God known" to your co-workers through your words and acts of charity. Remind yourself of one act or word that you will implement each day of the work-week. At the end of the week, assess your efforts and ask for the graces you need to be the Good News with your co-workers.

✧ In the Hebrew Scriptures, the elderly prophet Elijah places his mantle over the shoulders of his protégé, Elisha. When Elisha assumes the cloak, he feels its charge and impulse propelling him outward to bear witness to God's truth and compassion.
Have you ever experienced assuming the mantle of evangelization? Perhaps you have been moved by a talk you heard, a person you observed, a book you read, or a need you saw. Recall the power of this experience; stay with it. Converse with God about the graces you need to be renewed in your desire to spread the Good News.

✧ To prepare for this guided meditation about Jesus teaching, you may want to review the suggestions for using guided meditations, given in the foreword of this book:

In the presence of your Holy Friend, relax your whole body, starting with your feet and finishing with your head. . . . Breathe deeply and slowly, welcoming the breath of life and the Spirit of God. . . .

Now walk behind Jesus and his disciples to the synagogue at Nazareth. . . . A reverent hush greets the entrance of Jesus. . . . You take a seat in the back row, but you can see Jesus and his motley crew of followers. . . . A row of elders sits in front. . . . The leader of the synagogue walks up to Jesus and hands him the Torah. . . . Jesus slowly opens it and finds the text from Isaiah that he wants. . . . He rises, looks around at the assembly, takes a deep breath, and then reads firmly but distinctly this text:

> "The Spirit of the Lord is on me,
> for he has anointed me
> to bring the good news to the afflicted.
> He has sent me to proclaim liberty to captives,
> sight to the blind,
> to let the oppressed go free,
> to proclaim a year of favour from the Lord."
>
> (Luke 4:18–19)

Jesus hands the Scriptures back to a young attendant and begins to scan the room with his eyes. . . . His eyes stop and look into yours. . . . He says very deliberately, "Today, these words have been fulfilled in your hearing. . . ." Then he walks silently out of the synagogue. . . .

In the silence, you ponder his words to you. When you are ready, open your eyes.

Many people find it helpful to write down their reactions to guided meditations in a journal.

God's Word

Thanks be to God who always gives us in Christ a part in his triumphal procession, and through us is spreading everywhere the fragrance of the knowledge of himself. To

God we are the fragrance of Christ, both among those who are being saved and among those who are on the way to destruction. . . . At least we do not adulterate the word of God, as so many do, but it is in all purity, as envoys of God and in God's presence, that we speak in Christ. (2 Corinthians 2:14–15,17)

Closing prayer: With Samuel the prophet, I ask, "Send me, O God!" Send me to do your work in this world, and let me know you as I try to do it.

✧ Meditation 6 ✧

The Special Presence of Christ in the Poor

Theme: Vincent encountered Jesus Christ most powerfully among sick, abandoned, and hungry people—the outcasts of society.

Opening prayer: Gracious Jesus, open my eyes. Allow me to see you living within the poor people of this world. Let me meet you as I meet them. May I embrace you as I embrace them, learn from you as I learn from them.

About Vincent

Over the years, Vincent's method of assisting poor and needy people followed a definite four-step pattern. First, he identified a need. Second, he sent a small group of helpers, and then built up a financial base to expand the help. Finally, Vincent wrote directives about why and how to maintain the service. Many aspects of Vincent's spirituality can be found in the details of these manuals about working with poor people.

In one directory about working with abandoned children, Vincent describes details such as when to put the children to bed and get them up, how to avoid playing favorites, and the best way to correct the children. He also instructs the caretakers about how they are to look upon the children. He told them that just before they wake the children

> [the caregivers] shall kneel down and offer up to God all the services they are about to render the infancy of Our Lord in the person of these little children, and shall recite the *Veni Sancte Spiritus*. (Coste, *Life and Works*, vol. 2, p. 267)

Vincent composed another manual for the Daughters of Charity who cared for the convicts condemned to row in the French war galleys. The book is filled with practical instructions about how to remain safe and yet minister effectively. Folded into the details, Vincent reminds the Daughters that even though the convicts are hardened criminals, they still bear the presence of "Him who made Himself a slave to redeem us from the servitude of the evil one" (Coste, *Life and Works*, vol. 2, p. 322). Even if the convicts proved insolent or turned violent, the Sisters were to treat them with respect, because even these convicts carried the suffering Jesus within themselves.

Pause: Consider this: Do I really pay attention to Jesus' presence in hungry people, in panhandlers, in runaway kids, in homeless people?

Vincent's Words

> I should not judge poor peasants, men or women, by their exterior nor by their apparent mental capacities. All the more is this so since very frequently they scarcely seem to have the appearance or intelligence of reasonable beings, so gross and offensive are they. But turn the medal, and you will see by the light of faith that the Son of God, whose will it was to be poor, is represented to us by these people. (*Documents*, vol. 11, p. 32)

> Let us go then, my brothers, and work with a new love in the service of the poor, looking even for the most destitute and abandoned among them. Let us recognize that before

God they are our lords and masters and we are unworthy
to render them our small services. (*Documents*, vol. 11,
p. 393)

Let us, my sisters, cherish the poor as our masters, since
Our Lord is in them and they in Our Lord. (*Documents*,
vol. 13, p. 540)

Reflection

Seeing and attending figure prominently in prayer. Jesus chided those people who *look*, but do not really *see* because of their
prejudices, ignorance, or cynicism. Vincent did his seeing
through the eyes of the poor people with whom he worked.
They became the lenses through which he glimpsed God at
work in the world. Forsaken people, worthy in themselves,
were the holy ground where Vincent encountered the living
God.

Seeing and attending to God happen not only in quiet recollection but also in human exchanges, particularly with
God's poor. After all, prayer has been called a long, loving
look at the real. Orphans, victims of war, famine, and disease
present realities that can shake us out of our complacency or
feelings of self-sufficiency. They remind us that the suffering
Jesus is in our midst, that the Reign of God demands our attention, that only God can finally fill our hunger.

To see God's presence demands faith, faith that helps us
see beyond the ragged clothes, open sores, runny noses, gaunt
looks, angry attitude, sallow skin, or feigned indifference that
people may have. As Vincent said, "you will see by the light of
faith that the Son of God, whose will it was to be poor, is represented to us by these creatures." The reward of faith is an
encounter with the God of love.

✧ Recall your last encounter with a homeless or poor
person. What was your first reaction? What other feelings
arose within you? Were you conscious of God's presence in
the interaction? If so, how?

✧ This week as you read the newspaper and watch TV news programs, pay special attention to the ways in which these media portray poor people, homeless people, victims of war, people with AIDS. Try to note, perhaps in your journal, the attitudes displayed in the various programs. At the end of the week, evaluate the treatment of God's *anawim* in these media. Then ask yourself: How have I been influenced by these treatments of God's poor people? Is my view that of Christ or that of "the world"? Hold up your reactions before God.

✧ Pray slowly these words of Vincent's: "Turn the medal, and you will see by the light of faith that the Son of God, whose will it was to be poor, is represented to us by these people." Then recall any occasion during which you have seen below the surface and caught a glimpse of God's presence in a poor, sick, or abandoned person. Give thanks to God for this visitation.

✧ Read the story of the good Samaritan from Luke 10:29–37. Ponder each element of the story. Then pray over these questions:
✦ Who are the people that I have seen lately lying wounded in the ditch?
✦ What could I have done for them?
✦ What did I do?
Bring these people before God in prayer.

✧ To help his companions develop the habit of remembering God's presence in the abandoned children, Vincent composed a prayer that they should say each day. Compose your own prayer that will remind you of God's presence in poor people, in your co-workers, in all people. Offer this prayer during the first moments of your work day, and perhaps again at noon. Then, each evening for a week or two, ask yourself: Did I treat people as other Christs today?

God's Word

At the last judgment, the risen Christ will say to those on his right hand: "Come, you have been blessed by God with the inheritance prepared for you from the time of creation. For I was hungry, and you fed me. I thirsted, and you provided me with something to drink. I felt myself an alien, but you showed me hospitality. I had no clothes, you gave me garments. I was ill, and you nursed me to health. I had been tossed into prison, but you came to visit me."

The righteous will ask Christ: "But when did we do all these acts of charity and righteousness to you?"

And Jesus will declare, "In truth, when you did these things to any one of the least of your sisters or brothers, you did them to me." (Adapted from Matthew 25:34–40)

Closing prayer: Loving God, let me see into the eyes of sick people, prisoners, those who are hungry and thirsty, and when I do, may I see you there, suffering in solidarity with them. Change my way of seeing; then strengthen my will to act with justice and charity.

✧ **Meditation 7** ✧

Loving God in Heart and Deed

Theme: Christian love weaves together deep affection and hard work. It is an eminently practical passion.

Opening prayer: God, source of all oneness, bring my heart and my hands together. Let my love grow in action as much as in ardor. Teach me to serve you with the light of my mind, the heat of my feelings, and the strength of my body.

About Vincent

Vincent's affection for his brother priests was so well known that he could call them to task and not lose their love. He often corrected clergy who grumbled over duties that they thought were beneath the dignity of their calling.

One evening, reacting to some griping about his taking charge of a public hospital, he chided them in plain speech:

> Aren't the poor the suffering members of our Lord? Aren't they our brothers and sisters? If priests abandon them, who do you want to look after them? If there are any here who thought they joined this congregation only to preach the gospel to the poor but not to comfort them,

only to supply their spiritual needs but not their material ones, to them I say this. We should assist the poor in every way and do it both by ourselves and by enlisting the help of others. . . . To do this is to preach the gospel by works and by work. (*Documents*, vol. 12, p. 87)

Getting their hands dirty in the service of God's people was anything but demeaning. On the contrary, it made the Gospel real.

On another occasion, Vincent confronted some clerics who felt that the quality of their prayer experience took precedence over people's needs. Vincent told them:

So very often, many outpourings of affection for God, of resting in his presence, of good feelings toward everyone and sentiments and prayers like these, although very good and very desirable, are nonetheless suspect if they do not express themselves in practical love which has real effects. (*Documents*, vol. 11, p. 40)

Vincent, the realist, questioned any love that did not translate into deeds. Love had to be measured not just by the intensity of its yearning but by the efficacy of its results.

Pause: Ponder this question: To what extent does my desire to love and serve stay only in the realm of intention?

Vincent's Words

Let us love God, my brothers, let us love God. But let it be with the strength of our arms and the sweat of our brow. (*Documents*, vol. 11, p. 40)

We must pass, my sisters, from affective love to effective love. And that is a love which takes flesh in works of charity, service of the poor which is undertaken with joy, constancy and tender love. (*Documents*, vol. 11, p. 593)

The Congregation took Christ the Lord as a model, as someone who did not begin by teaching but by doing. . . . It is equally necessary to point out that he is a model also for doing all things well, because whatever good we may do deserves blame rather than praise if it is not done well. (*Constitutions*, p. 150)

Reflection

Vincent would not pit prayer against deeds of charity, or practical plans against affective responses to God's love. Authentic Christian love integrates intellect, affections, and action.

In Vincent's mind, religious fervor did not exclude intelligence. Effective service to God's needy people had to be done competently, not just fervently. It had to actually help. On the other hand, he knew that charity could slacken if it was not constantly strengthened through prayer and discernment with God. Vincent brought his needs and questions about his work to his prayer.

Though not articulated in the language of the twentieth century, Vincent in his own way acknowledged the connections between oppressive structures in society and the straits of poor people. He often spoke about the "maxims of the world and the maxims of the Gospel," realizing fully that the two were many times not compatible. Individual charity not only meant serving poor people, but also setting up new structures of service and reforming the social fabric to reflect more fully the values of the Gospel. Ever practical, Vincent tried to be not only an affective evangelizer, but also an effective one.

✧ Pray repeatedly these words of Vincent's: "Let us love God. . . . But let it be with the strength of our arms and the sweat of our brow." As you pray, picture instances when you did love God in actions of charity and justice.

✧ Recall two sincere attempts that you made to be helpful to someone else, one of which worked and the other which did not. Before God, reflect on the any differences between the two acts of charity.

✧ Dialog with Jesus about these questions:

✦ Are there any situations that have moved me to feel deep compassion, but about which I have taken no action or been moved "from *affective* love to *effective* love" (to use Vincent's words)?

✦ What can I do to put my love into action?

✦ Do any fears or weaknesses or prejudices block my taking charitable action?

✦ What help do I need from God to move from affective love to effective love?

✧ To be effective in loving service requires knowledge and skill. Meditate on these words of the Scriptures: "You must love your God with all your heart, with all your soul, with all your strength, and with all your mind, and your neighbor as yourself" (Luke 10:27).

Then reflect on this question: Knowing my limitations and talents, what knowledge and skills could I acquire that would help me love my sisters and brothers more effectively?

✧ Act. Contribute time and energy to the service of someone who needs your help, or to some justice or peace-making effort.

God's Word

How does it help . . . when someone who has never done a single good act claims to have faith? Will that faith bring salvation? If one of the brothers or one of the sisters is in need of clothes and has not enough food to live on, and one of you says to them, "I wish you well; keep yourself warm and eat plenty," without giving them these bare necessities of life, then what good is that? In the same way faith: if good deeds do not go with it, it is quite dead. (James 2:14–17)

Closing prayer:

Lord Jesus, teach me by your example. . . . Make me, through the vigor of my efforts, set the world around me on fire. I want to give myself to you, body and soul, heart and mind and spirit so that I may always do what gladdens you. In your mercy, grant me the grace to have you continue in me and through me your saving work. (*Documents,* vol. 11, pp. 74–75)

✧ Meditation 8 ✧

The Cultivation of Virtue

Theme: To be apostles of Jesus Christ, Christians must cultivate and nurture the virtues necessary to carry out their mission.

Opening prayer: Strengthen my will, God, my rock, that I may cultivate the virtues essential to Christian life. Send your grace, without which I can do nothing.

About Vincent

In 1618, the young Vincent met Francis de Sales. This reform-minded bishop attracted Vincent because of his sunny disposition, self-possession, wisdom, ease in human relationships, and gentleness. Vincent marveled at De Sales's approachability and obvious self-discipline, and became aware of the contrasts with his own character. People had often reproved Vincent for his harsh, almost driven streak, and commented about his steep mood swings. Defensive, Vincent would argue that he was the way he was and could not change.

However, soon after his meeting with the saintly and admired De Sales, Vincent traveled to a monastery outside of Paris for his annual retreat. The meeting with De Sales permeated his reflections. During the retreat he finally stared honestly at his aggressive edges and his tendency to depression.

During one intense period of prayer, Vincent threw himself on God's mercy, recognizing at last that only God's power could calm his harshness and ease his sharp mood swings. At the same time, he acknowledged that the process of conversion would also involve a large dose of self-discipline. Many years later, Vincent recounted this crucial moment:

> I turned to God and earnestly begged him to convert this irritable and forbidding trait of mine. I also asked for a kind and amiable spirit. And with the grace of Our Lord, by giving a little attention to checking the hot-blooded impulses of my personality, I have been at least partly cured of my gloomy disposition. (Louis Abelly, *The Life of Vincent de Paul*, vol. 3, pp. 177–178)

God's grace empowered Vincent to change his ways. His response led to personal asceticism.

Pause: Ask yourself this: In what areas of my life do I tend not to be as self-disciplined as I might be in responding to God's promptings?

Vincent's Words

Vincent opens his one book of spiritual teachings to the Congregation of the Mission with this principle:

> We read in the sacred scripture that our Lord, Jesus Christ, sent on earth for the salvation of the human race, did not begin by teaching; he began by doing. And what he did was to integrate fully into his life every type of virtue. . . . Now the little Congregation wants, with God's grace, to imitate Christ, the Lord, in so far as that is possible in view of its limitations. It seeks to imitate his virtues. . . . (*Constitutions*, p. 105)

Typical of Vincent's encouragements to virtue is the following recommendation about learning to be genuine and yet discreet:

> Christ recommends the simplicity of a dove, and he tells us to have the prudence of a serpent as well. What he

means is that we should speak and behave with discretion. . . . In actual practice this virtue is about choosing the right way to do things. We should make it a sacred principle, then, admitting of no exceptions, that since we are working for God we will always choose God-related ways for carrying out our work, and see and judge things from Christ's point of view and not from a worldly-wise one; . . . That is how we can be prudent as serpents and simple as doves. (*Constitutions*, pp. 109–110)

Reflection

To Vincent, a life of virtue was no accident. God gives the grace, but human effort is required to cultivate the virtue. Habits of charity, hopefulness, and justice are *built*, not just wished into being.

Vincent was not encouraging stoicism, a training regimen of difficult acts repeated over and over to develop spiritual muscle. He did not portray the prototype Christian as an iron-willed person who could withstand all pressures in carrying out his or her Christian duty.

On the other hand, Vincent knew that good intentions were insufficient responses to God's grace too. Virtue—a good habit, an inner readiness to accomplish moral good—had to become part of the fabric of life. He would certainly have agreed with this wise saying:

Plant an act; reap a habit.
Plant a habit; reap a virtue.
Plant a virtue; reap a character.
Plant a character; reap a destiny.

Reflected-upon action, repeated intentionally, becomes a habitual channeling of religious energy. For instance, by acting patiently over and over in certain trying situations, a person may learn patience. Virtues such as patience are important in the full living of the Christian life.

Vincent constantly made concrete suggestions about how to develop virtue. From hard experience, he knew that definite dispositions had to be cultivated into the heart of the servant if the Gospels were to come alive through his or her hands.

✧ Examine your own consciousness. Write an assessment of the ways in which you have cultivated key Christian virtues in your life. Ask yourself how you have developed and are developing these virtues: charity, prudence, fortitude, justice, and temperance.

✧ If an intimate friend of yours was writing an "apostolic assessment" on you, what weaknesses and strengths in certain virtues would he or she tell about you. Imagine that the two of you are sitting down together to discuss the performance review. You begin by asking your friend: "Thanks for being willing to do this apostolic assessment with me. Start with my weaknesses or my lack of development in certain virtues."

After you have asked this initial question, role-play your conversation in your mind: your friend says something, then you respond with a question or comment. Talk about your virtues and your weaknesses. You might even ask for ideas about ways to reinforce your strengths.

End your discussion by praying together for the graces you need to cultivate virtue in your life.

Many people find it helpful to write out such a dialog.

✧ The late Dag Hammarskjöld, secretary-general of the United Nations, knew that deep trust in God did not excuse him from trying to translate that trust into action. Meditate on his counsel for vigilance and virtue.

> You cannot play with the animal in you
> without becoming wholly animal,
> play with falsehood
> without forfeiting your right to truth,
> play with cruelty
> without losing your sensitivity of mind.
> He who wants to keep his garden tidy
> doesn't reserve a plot for weeds.
>
> (*Markings*, p. 15)

✧ Dietrich Bonhoeffer was a Lutheran pastor who was murdered by the Nazis for his part in resistance activities in Germany during World War II. He wholeheartedly believed that God freely gives us grace, but Bonhoeffer also knew that such grace demands a price. Pray slowly these words of his:

> Cheap grace is the preaching of forgiveness without requiring repentance, baptism without church discipline, Communion without confession, absolution without personal confession. Cheap grace is grace without discipline, grace without the cross, grace without Jesus Christ, living and incarnate. (*The Cost of Discipleship*, p. 37)

God's Word

Let love be without any pretense. Avoid what is evil; stick to what is good. . . . Let your feelings of deep affection for one another come to expression and regard others as more important than yourself. In the service of [God], work not half-heartedly but with conscientiousness and an eager spirit. Be joyful in hope, persevere in hardship; keep praying regularly; share with any of God's holy people who are in need; look for opportunities to be hospitable. (Romans 12:9–13)

Closing prayer:

Jesus Christ my Savior,
during your life here on earth
you practiced charity and the support of others
incomparably more than anyone else. . . .

Let my practice of these virtues
contribute to the realization of God's designs,
so that through imitating you
I may glorify God,
and by my example lead others to his service.

(Braakhuis, *Praying*, no. 7)

Humility

Theme: Vincent recognized that all of his successes, talents, and works came from the grace that God alone provided. Recognizing our complete dependence on God is the beginning of humility.

Opening prayer: Gracious God, may I see myself as you see me, and may I fully acknowledge that all that I am is a pure gift from you. Make me one who freely gives back what you have given me—everything.

About Vincent

Some of Vincent's contemporaries thought him a bit odd for always talking about himself disparagingly. He sprinkled conversations with self-deprecating asides. His listeners knew that he was not just trying to attract attention. Vincent had no doubts that any good that he did flowed from God's goodness. This conviction permeated Vincent and the organization that he founded.

Once, one of his missionaries sent Vincent a pamphlet that the missionary had been asked to write. The document recounted the many accomplishments of Vincent's institute in France. The priest thought that Vincent would enjoy seeing the pamphlet and might respond with a few words of appreciation. The missionary badly miscalculated.

Vincent judged the publication to be thoroughly inappropriate. He dashed off a sharp note to the priest:

> I am so upset by your pamphlet that I can hardly find the words to tell you why. . . . It is absolutely opposed to humility to broadcast what we are and what we do. . . . If there is anything good in us and in our way of life, that good comes from God. It is up to God to let that be known. . . . As for us poor and flawed workers, our task is more to hide ourselves. We are people who on our own cannot bring off anything good, people who should not even be thought about. That is why I have refused all along to let publicity go out that would cause us to be lionized by anyone. (*Documents*, vol. 6, pp. 176–177)

Vincent feared that success would slowly blind him to the truth of his and the congregation's reliance on God.

Pause: Consider this: In what ways do I regard myself as self-created, as the origin of the good that I do—on a kind of par with God?

Vincent's Words

In many letters to members of his congregation, Vincent revealed how centrally he regarded humility:

> Let us stop saying, "It is I who have done this work." For every good thing ought to be done in the name of our Lord Jesus Christ. (*Documents*, vol. 7, pp. 98–99)

> Be wary about crediting anything to yourself. In claiming this, you in effect steal from God and do him injury. God alone is the author of every good thing. (*Documents*, vol. 7, p. 289)

> God pours out his inexhaustible gifts on the humble, those who recognize that all the good done by them comes from God. (*Documents*, vol. 11, pp. 56–57)

Humility is the virtue of Jesus Christ, the virtue of his holy mother, the virtue of the greatest of the saints, and finally it is the virtue of missionaries. (*Documents*, vol. 11, pp. 56–57)

In a shared prayer session, Vincent stated:

To become more humble means choosing to take the lowest place, opting to place ourselves below the least of the brothers and sisters. . . . We are instinctively repelled by these kinds of things. Yet we must overcome this distaste. We have to make especially strong efforts to put this virtue into actual practice. Otherwise, it will never develop inside us. (*Documents*, vol. 11, pp. 54–55)

Reflection

God loves a cheerful giver, but God also loves a thankful receiver. At the core of humility is a profound sense that God has given us everything that is good. Humility allows us to see all as gift. So we rejoice, not in our own doing, but in God's bounty. For instance, Mary sang with her whole being in appreciation to God because of what the saving God did for her. She glories in her reliance on God. Her proclaimed "lowliness" does not cancel out her worth at all. Rather, she celebrates that God loves and blesses her as she is—a simple human being undeserving of such tremendous love. Humility and thankfulness move in tandem.

Vincent learned humility from the poor people that he served. In their own lowliness, many of them had discovered Mary's gratitude. Unlike people of plenty, poor people experienced raw, immediate need. They knew what it meant to receive their daily bread. Some turned bitter, but others gave thanks and blessings. Out of the sharpness of their need, they grew thankful for God's often ignored wonders: a crust of bread, clean water, perhaps an apple. The gratefulness of poor people served as a constant reminder to Vincent that even the simple gifts are still gifts from the God who loves us.

✧ In a column on one side of a piece of paper, write a list of all of your accomplishments like the priest in the section "About Vincent." Then reread Vincent's answer to the priest as if it were written to you. Be aware of your feelings. Meditate on your feelings about his words to you.

Then, next to each accomplishment, acknowledge what talents, skills, or other gifts made the achievement possible. Thank God for giving you the ability to do what you did. Allow yourself to be amazed at God's empowerment.

✧ Recall an occasion during which you felt that your life was an awesome gift. Perhaps it was a time when a special person said she or he loved you. Maybe you had a close call, when you kept thinking "it all could have been so different." Re-enact this moment of blessing. Let your imagination set the scene, invite the actors to play the scene, participate just as you did. Permit your feelings to emerge. Then, speak with God about this time of giftedness.

✧ Is there a situation in your life right now that you find humiliating? How can this situation be a call from God to continuing conversion? What attitude could you bring to this situation so that it could become freeing and empowering for you? Then thank God for this and other parts of your life that you find humbling.

✧ Picture yourself sitting in a room of Zechariah's home on the morning Mary comes to visit Elizabeth. You watch them embrace and begin talking. Mary's face lights up as she listens to Elizabeth. Hang on each of Mary's words:

> My being proclaims your greatness
> and my spirit finds joy in you, God my Savior.
> For you have looked upon me, your servant, in my
> lowliness;
> all ages to come shall call me blessed.
> God, you who are mighty, have done great things for me.
> Holy is your name.
>
> (Adapted from Luke 1:46–49)

Then in the silence of your heart, pray these same words, pondering all the great things God has done for you. As you recall each gift, pray with Mary, "Holy is your name."

✧ Meditatively read the "God's Word" section of this meditation. Consider what a wonderful blessing it is that God became a human being just like you. Then ponder what your crosses are and will be—the crosses you carry for love. Thank God for your humanity and for the crosses carried in obedience to the call to love.

God's Word

Make your own the mind of Christ Jesus:
Who, being in the form of God,
did not count equality with God
something to be grasped.

But he emptied himself,
taking the form of a slave,
becoming as human beings are;
and being in every way like a human being,
he was humbler yet,
even to accepting death, death on a cross.

And for this God raised him high,
and gave him the name
which is above all other names.

(Philippians 2:5–9)

Closing prayer:

O Blessed Virgin Mary,
in your *Magnificat* you stated
that Almighty God had done great things for you
because of your humility
on which he had looked with favor.

True practice of humility
is in obedience to God's will.

My Lord and my Savior,
with all the tenderness of my love for you
I humbly ask you for that virtue.

Holy Virgin,
help me obtain that grace from your Son;
I hope that, through your intercession,
I may always have the sincere desire
to be outstanding in my humble obedience to God's will
as you always were.

(Braakhuis, *Praying*, no. 19)

Truthful Simplicity

Theme: Vincent believed that facing and speaking the unvarnished truth were requisites for one who would proclaim the Gospels fully.

Opening prayer: Jesus, in your earthly life and death, you showed us how to speak in truth and simplicity. Grant me the grace to be honest with myself. May your truth grow so powerful in me that it excludes easy, tempting half-truths. Then help me to openly, honestly, and courageously proclaim your Word.

About Vincent

Once during Vincent's seminary days, his father unexpectedly paid him a visit. Embarrassed by his humble origins, Vincent had concealed his background. He had not told his classmates that his parents were farmers. So when the porter announced that a plainly dressed man had come to the door claiming to be Vincent's father, Vincent feigned confusion. He instructed the porter that evidently some mistake had been made and the man should be sent away.

Fifty years later Vincent painfully recounted this incident during a conference he was giving about simplicity. He confessed that he had learned about the damage such duplicity could cause. Jesus, Vincent told his listeners, spoke simply and clearly because God wanted everyone to know the truth. Besides, if God's ministers shaded the facts and gave hints of hidden agendas, people could hardly be expected to listen when they preached God's word.

In a letter to one of the priests of his congregation, Vincent re-emphasized the need for truthful simplicity:

> You know that your own kind heart has given me, thanks be to God, full liberty to speak to you with the utmost confidence, without any concealment or disguise; and it seems to me that up to the present you have recognized that fact in all my dealings with you. My God! Am I to fall into the misfortune of being forced to do or to say, in my dealings with you, anything contrary to holy simplicity? Oh! Sir! May God preserve me from doing so in regard to anything whatsoever! It is a virtue I love most, the one to which in all my actions I pay most heed, so it seems to me; and if it were lawful to say so, the one, I may say, in which I have, by God's mercy, made some progress. (*Documents*, vol. 1, p. 284)

Pause: Ponder this question: Have I ever felt the strength of God flowing through me when I needed to speak a costly truth?

Vincent's Words

> Jesus, the Lord, expects us to have the simplicity of a dove. This means giving a straightforward opinion about things in the way we honestly see them, without needless reservations. It also means doing things without any double-dealing or manipulation, our intention being focused solely on God. Each of us, then, should take care to behave always in this spirit of simplicity, remembering that God likes to deal with the simple, and that he conceals the secrets of heaven from the wise and prudent of this world and reveals them to little ones. (*Constitutions*, p. 109)

> Everyone feels an attraction for persons who are simple and candid, persons who refuse to employ cunning or de-

ceit. They are popular because they act ingenuously, and speak sincerely; their lips are ever in accord with their hearts. They are esteemed and loved everywhere. (*Documents*, vol. 12, p. 171)

Reflection

Under the pressures of complex dealings with politicians, landlords, magistrates, ambassadors, church officials, philanthropists, and nobles of his day, Vincent increasingly appreciated the simplicity that Jesus spoke of. Political intrigue, dissimulation, cunning, and political intrigue repelled Vincent.

Vincent sought to imitate Jesus, who spoke plainly and with special concern for simple people. Straightforward speech and unpretentious action manifested God's love clearly and effectively. The people of God should never be manipulated.

✧ Select one line from the two passages in the "Vincent's Words" section and meditate on it. By repeating it in your mind, allow its meaning to become clearer.

✧ Recall a time when you shaved some of the truth from your words in order to save appearances.
✦ What thoughts and fears registered within you at the time?
✦ How did you feel after your dissimulation?
✦ Why did you feel the need to lie?
✦ Did your dissimulation really solve anything?

✧ Ponder Shakespeare's famous counsel:

This above all: to thine own self be true.
And it must follow, as the night the day,
Thou canst not be false to any man. (*Hamlet*, 1, 3)

In your journal, write your reflections on these questions:
✦ What about myself do I find most difficult to be "true" about?
✦ In what situations do I find myself varnishing the truth?

✦ Do I love myself sufficiently to be "true" or do I have to hide who I really am out of shame or envy?
Ask God for the graces that you need to be true to yourself.

✧ Bring to mind someone you have admired for his or her passionate commitment to speaking and living truthfully. Recall instances during which you saw this person's honesty revealed. What did you feel in the presence of such truthfulness? When you think of this person, what comparable stories of Jesus' honesty come to mind? Pray for this person, and ask God to bless you with the same grace of truthfulness.

✧ Recall a time when you spoke the truth in the face of your own fears. Remember who was there, what was involved, what you said, and the results of your words. Write an account of this incident and what you learned from it.

✧ If you have been giving someone half-truths or have been manipulating someone, try to bring the light of truth to the situation. Ask yourself why you dissembled or manipulated. Pray that God will help you make things right. Go to the person and attempt to put your relationship on an honest footing.

✧ Pray repeatedly the words: "Jesus, truth of God among us, help me to live in the truth."

God's Word

Jesus said:
If you make my word your home
you will indeed be my disciples;
you will come to know the truth,
and the truth will set you free.

(John 8:31–32)

Closing prayer: Jesus, light and truth of God, touch my heart with passion for the truth. May my words be plain. May my intentions be pure. Set me free with your saving truth.

Dying to Self

Theme: Service to God's people demands a price. Christians must put aside their own prejudices, comfortable circumstances, and favorite ideas in order to do the will of God. This sort of discipline calls Christians to die to themselves in order to follow Christ. Vincent called this discipline *mortification.*

Opening prayer: Jesus, you prayed, lived, and died so that God's will would be done. You embraced the demands of love and prophecy to bring the Reign of God. Grant that I may have a lighter hold on the things I have. Help me to leave behind those things that enslave me and hold me from doing your will. May I die to all that stands between me and the service of your people.

About Vincent

Mortification, or dying to self, did not remain theoretical to Vincent. In the school of service, Vincent paid the price of his commitment to doing God's will.

While Vincent was still a young man, his yearning to serve poor people grew rapidly. However, his repugnance in their presence did not match his enthusiasm. Poor people made him queasy. Vincent had to discipline himself not to forsake his good intentions.

In 1618, the bishop of Paris asked for volunteers to care for the galley slaves held in naval prisons. These prisons were corruptly administered, foul smelling, ridden with disease, lethally dangerous—the most horrendous prisons of the day. Being a prisoner there was slow capital punishment. Nevertheless, Vincent volunteered to minister to these prisoners.

Swallowing his revulsion and suppressing his fear, Vincent moved among the prisoners, dressing their wounds, sharing their meals, and teaching the Gospel. For days on end, he spread compassion and brought light to prisoners thrown into living hell.

Vincent realized that ministry to the prisoners, indeed ministry to any of God's poor people, required that he die to his attachment to pleasant fragrances, tasty meals, clean linens, polite conversation, and even personal safety.

One of the most stunning compliments Vincent ever gave was to a young woman who practiced such detachment. Barbara Angiboust ministered in the prisons, and died from a contagion that ravaged the jail population. Long after her death, Vincent pointed to her as a shining example of dying to self in order to serve humanity. He would tell of Barbara Angiboust carrying heavy pots of steaming stew among the cursing inmates of the galleys. Sometimes fights would break out when Angiboust tried to feed the inmates, and when she attempted to bring peace to the jostling mob, the hot stew would spill over her hands. She would say nothing, but as she left, she would whisper words of forgiveness. Often she intervened when warders started beating the same prisoners who treated her so crudely.

Vincent knew that Barbara Angiboust could serve the prisoners because she had died to her own whims and compulsions. To her companion Daughters of Charity, Vincent remarked:

> Suppose there is a sister who is tempted to keep something for herself. As soon as she feels this selfish impulse, she must work against it. And if it persists in trying to wear her down, she should give it a slap on the nose and make it keep silent. (*Documents*, vol. 10, p. 58)

Pause: Ask yourself: To what extent has my love of my neighbor stretched me, moved me out of my comfort zone, worked a change in my habits?

Vincent's Words

Counseling a group of missionaries who preached throughout rural France, Vincent told them:

> When we go on a mission, we do not know where we will stay or exactly what we shall be doing. We will have to adjust to things we never expected, for Providence frequently upsets our plans. Who then does not see that mortification has to be an integral part of the missionary not only in his dealings with the poor but also in his service to those making a retreat, to seminarians, to convicts and to slaves? Because if we are not mortified, how can we put up with what has to be endured in these different works? (*Documents*, vol. 12, pp. 307–308)

Reflection

Mortification, or dying to self, has sometimes become confused with self-hate, repression, antagonism between body and soul, justification by works, masochism, or codependency. The concept of mortification fights a negative history. However, dying to self is a core value in the Christian Testament.

Vincent studied Luke's Gospel, which outlines the conditions of discipleship: "Whosoever would be my disciples must detach themselves from their parents, spouses and children, siblings, and even life itself. If you are not willing to carry the cross and follow me, you cannot be my follower" (adapted from Luke 14:26–27). The apostles had to die to their old habits of mind and action to follow Jesus, who invited them into new ways of seeing themselves and into a new mission. Without mortification, the apostles could not be free and become healers and preachers of the Good News.

After all, followers of Jesus may have to take leave of the values of their parents, loved ones, employers, and culture. Peacemaking means dying to violent answers to conflicts. Acting justly sometimes demands opposing strongly held positions of the majority of society. In short, Christians have to embrace mortification to love as Jesus does.

Vincent believed that mortification had to be a conscious choice. With the grace of God, people could be willing to make the hard sacrifices that love demands. With God's help, they could detach themselves from—or die to—all that was not Christ so that they could put on Jesus Christ (see Colossians 3:9–15).

✦ In the "Vincent's Words" section, he says: "We do not know where we will stay or exactly what we shall be doing. We will have to adjust to things we never expected, for Providence frequently upsets our plans." Recall some recent instances when your plans were upset or when you had to adjust to things you never expected. How did you react? How did you feel in each instance?

Then reflect on these questions:

✦ Do I expect to be in control most of the time?
✦ What is God telling me when my plans are upset and I have to adjust to the unexpected?
✦ Talk honestly with God about your response to the unexpected or your need to control.

✦ Reread the passage from Luke quoted in the "Reflection" section. Make a list of attachments, indulgences, compulsions, narrow habits of mind and action from which you need to detach yourself in order to freely serve God and your neighbor. Make a "Plan of Detachment" that will help you gradually—one day at a time—free yourself from one of these indulgences, compulsions, or habits. Realizing that only God's grace brings freedom, ask God for the graces you need to free yourself from those things that prevent you from serving God and your sisters and brothers.

✦ List your "crosses"—the aspects of your life that are trying, confusing, or demanding of self-sacrifice and dying to self.

Which of these crosses are a burden because they are part of love, justice, or peacemaking? Ask God's grace to help you carry these crosses.

Are any of these crosses self-inflicted: that is, are any of these burdens the result of self-indulgence, compulsions, ignorance, or carelessness? Ask God's grace to help you discard these crosses and change your life so that you will have room for love, justice, and peace.

✧ Read the story of Jesus' agony in the Garden of Gethsemane (Mark 14:32–42) or bring it to mind. See Jesus kneeling in the darkened Garden. Hear the insects and the rustling of the trees. Listen carefully as Jesus says, "Abba, you can do anything. Please take this cup from me. But, above all, let your will be done." Imagine the expression on Jesus' face and the flood of his feelings.

In the garden with Jesus, pray the same prayer. Ask God to take away any "cups" that you do not think you can drink, and then submit to God's holy will.

✧ Identify one area of your life which could be simplified to free some of your money or time for service of your neighbor. Take action. Simplify. Take what money you save and share it with people in need. Take what time you save and share it with lonely, sick, imprisoned, or homebound people.

God's Word

You must die to . . . sexual perversity, unchecked passions, evil desires, and greed in particular because it is like worshipping a false god. . . . Now you must replace anger, outbreaks of temper, malice, libelous and lurid talk, and lies. Strip off your old behavior as you strip off your old self. Put on the new person created in God's own image. . . . Christ is everything.

As God's chosen ones, the people God loves, clothe yourselves in profound compassion, abundant generosity, tenderness, and patience. Bear each other's burdens. Forgive each other just as God has forgiven you. For your cloak, put on love. (Adapted from Colossians 3:5–14)

Closing prayer:

O my Savior, you know what harm is done to a person by excessive attachments and desires. In your goodness, free me from them by giving me the virtue of detachment. . . . I am also praying for this now by all the sufferings you went through on earth, by the goodness of your Holy Mother, and through the intercession of all those who have entered the great joy of heaven through their practice of this virtue. (*Documents*, vol. 10, p. 708)

Zeal

Theme: Zeal for God's Reign must burn white-hot so that the word of God may spread and transform all of humankind.

Opening prayer: Passionate God, inflame my passion for your Gospel. Unsettle me with its urgency, move me with its power. May I be caught up in zeal to announce your presence and to act with love.

About Vincent

Vincent warned others against overtaxing their strength out of zeal for spreading the Good News; however, he did not always follow his own advice.

When Vincent was in his sixty-ninth year, a civil war known as the Fronde broke out all over France. Paris became an armed camp. Appalled by the suffering, Vincent watched his relief supplies dwindle precipitously as he attempted to help the war's victims.

Vincent resolved to try his own hand at mediation. On a bitterly cold January night, he and a companion left Paris on horseback and slipped through the encircling army's lines. A few miles outside the city's gates, the two men came to the ice-clogged River Seine, where they struggled across the ice to the Queen's encampment. The queen politely received Vincent and his companion, although she refused Vincent's plea to dismiss her chief minister, Cardinal Mazarin, as a first step to peace.

Not to be deterred so easily, Vincent visited Mazarin himself and asked the cardinal to step down. Even though Mazarin did not punish Vincent for his temerity, he dismissed Vincent from a high-level commission on religious affairs and spread the word that Vincent's star had fallen at court.

Recognizing that he could not accomplish anything with the queen and Mazarin, Vincent rode back through countryside that had been ravaged by passing armies. While fording another river, Vincent's horse stumbled, tossed him into the frigid current, and trapped him underneath its body. Vincent's companion rescued him, and they both limped off to a nearby inn where they dried out and spent a week recovering. Even in his weakened state, Vincent began teaching catechism to some of the other boarders—one day into his recuperation.

For the rest of the winter, Vincent, elderly by the standards of his day, traveled the length and breadth of western France, shoring up relief efforts and supervising the charitable societies he had founded.

Worn out at the end of winter, Vincent returned to Paris for a much needed rest. However, thousands of destitute refugees were lined up outside his door. All spring, he administered an emergency shelter and food bank set up at his headquarters.

Zeal burned in Vincent until the end. In the last year of his life, Vincent confided to some visitors:

> In spite of my age [79], I tell you before God that I do not feel excused from the responsibility of working for the salvation of the poor. For what could really get in the way of my doing that now? If I cannot preach every day, all right, I'll preach twice a week. If I cannot preach more important sermons, I will preach less important ones. If the congregation cannot hear me at a distance, what is to prevent me from speaking in an informal, more familiar way to those poor just as I am speaking to you right now? What is to hinder me from gathering them near me just as you are sitting around me now? (*Documents*, vol. 11, p. 136)

Pause: Ask yourself: Does zeal for God's Reign burn within me?

Vincent's Words

In one of his most memorable conferences, Vincent spoke on zeal:

> Zeal . . . is made up of a genuine desire to please God and to be useful to others: zeal for extending God's kingdom, zeal for achieving others' salvation. Is there anything in the whole world more perfect than this? If God's love is fire, then zeal is its flame; if God's love is a sun, zeal is its ray. Zeal is the purest element in loving God. (*Documents*, vol. 12, pp. 307–308)

Reflection

From experience, Vincent knew that fervor could go wrong. He often cautioned against "undisciplined enthusiasm," a false zeal that springs from desire for praise or from anger (*Constitutions*, p. 157). Unlike true zeal, compulsions take on a hard edge of self-righteousness or paralyzing preoccupation with self: what *I* do, rather than what *God* wants done.

True zeal sets a person on fire with love of God, with the realization that all gifts and all power come from God. Thus, true zeal is humble but courageous in the face of scorn and persecution. True zeal acts with charity, not out of a desire to manipulate, or out of trendy do-goodism. Christian zeal models itself on Jesus' zeal to proclaim the Good News of God's love and to heal the wounds of suffering people.

To discern the direction of his zeal, Vincent depended on the insights of his spiritual director, trusted friends, the response of the people he served, and the guidelines of his community. He wanted to make sure that the fire of his zeal came from the love of God and his sisters and brothers and not from a false sense of his own importance. The fire of Christian zeal warms and nurtures; it never destroys. Christian zeal creates, gives energy, and empowers. Vincent listened to those whom he trusted to be sure that his fire burned from the right source.

✧ Read the "Vincent's Words" section of this meditation again. Select a phrase that most applies to or challenges you. Reflect on it. Then converse with Jesus about ways you can be more zealous, like him.

✧ Right now, what sets you on fire? When do you experience zeal? To answer these questions, reflect on times in your life when you felt most alive, energized, when you radiated confidence that what you were about was good and meaningful, when you wished that you could hold the feelings for a lifetime.

✧ An especially important sign of zeal is fidelity. This is fervor and commitment to love, serve, or believe—stretched over the long haul. Reflect on some of the fidelities and infidelities of your life. Lift these up in gratitude or sorrow before an always faithful God. Ask for the grace you need to continue being faithful and for the gift of forgiveness for infidelities.

✧ Sit quietly. Relax. Close your eyes. Become aware of your breathing, letting yourself feel the air filling up and then escaping your lungs. When you have calmed yourself, begin on the inhale to pray the words "the love of Christ" and on the exhale the phrase, "urges me on." This verse from 2 Corinthians 5:14 is the motto Vincent gave to the Daughters of Charity.

✧ This meditation may help you touch God's fire. Remember that the call to Moses to free God's people from oppression is the call to all followers of Jesus Christ:

> First, relax. Get comfortable. Breathe slowly. If you need to, stretch your body. When you are ready, begin the journey of Moses up Mount Horeb.
>
> You walk up the mountain trail. . . . It is a long hike. . . . You come into a clearing. . . . Before you, a bush suddenly bursts into flame. . . . Even so, the bush is not consumed by the flames. . . . Then, from the middle of the flames, God calls your name twice. . . . You answer, "Here I am!". . . Then God tells you, "Take off your shoes, for the place where you are is holy ground." . . . You hastily remove your shoes. . . . God says, "I am the God of your ancestors. And I have seen the misery of my people in the world, in your city, and in your area. I have heard them crying. And I have come to save them. So I am sending you to lead my people to freedom, to truth, and to justice and peace." . . .
>
> You reply, "But, my God, what am I to do?" . . . "Look around you, my friend, who are the poor in your midst, who the sick, who the lonely, who in need?" . . . You ponder God's words to you. . . . Then you answer God's question. . . .
>
> You add, "But, God, I cannot help all these people!" . . . God answers, "True! What can you do?" . . . After reflecting, you reply, listing some of the good that you

can do. . . . God tells you, "Now go, I will help you all along the way. I will be with you." . . . Immediately the flames cease. . . . You rest for some moments, pondering this encounter with God. . . .

When you are ready, return from the mountain and open your eyes.

After this guided meditation, you might wish to write any reactions in your journal.

God's Word

Proof of God's love came when Jesus gave his life for us. Now we should lay down our lives for one another. How can God's love dwell within anyone who has many possessions but refuses to aid a brother or sister in need? (Adapted from 1 John 3:16–17)

Closing prayer:

O my God,
    set my heart on fire
    with the desire to serve you! . . .
As long as you lived in this world
    all your thoughts went out to the salvation of all
        people. . . .
Teach me by your example,
    grant me all the virtues proper to true evangelizers,
    and make me, through the fervor of my zeal,
    set the world around me on fire.
I want to give myself to you,
    body and soul,
    heart and mind and spirit,
    in order always to do what pleases you.
                          (Braakhuis, *Praying*, no. 29)

Strong Gentleness, Gentle Strength

Theme: The apostle's work requires a blend of firmness and gentleness. Knowing the right proportions for any situation is an art and a blessing.

Opening prayer: Jesus, your Reign comes through both gentleness and strength. Let me understand when to challenge and when to nurture, when to move with righteous anger and when to be tender.

About Vincent

For some years, Vincent sat on a high-level government council for religious affairs. This group often had to handle the always-sensitive episcopal nominations.

On one occasion, Vincent was given a letter from a well-known preacher, a member of a religious order, who had, "in all humility," nominated himself for a vacant diocese. The friar argued that the strain of keeping his order's rule depleted his energies and that his considerable gifts could be better used in the episcopacy. Vincent had the leverage to either be heavy-handed or just ignore the friar.

In his response, Vincent mixed firmness with gentleness, and not a little tongue-in-cheek humor. After telling the priest that he would undoubtedly do wonders as a bishop, Vincent delivered a mild rebuke by reminding him that the proper procedure was for someone else to spot episcopal talent and to submit the name. Vincent then pleads the case of the man's religious order, pointing out how devastating it would be for them to lose such a star. Finally, Vincent turns back the man's complaint about his lack of energy:

> Take my word for it, you should give up your exhausting work of preaching for a while and pay more attention to your health. Build it up. You still have a lot to give both God and your order. And after all, it *is* one of the holiest and most dynamic in the Church. (*Documents*, vol. 4, p. 19)

Message delivered, damage minimal. Both the truth and the man's feelings were served.

This instinct for wrapping firmness in gentleness proved itself effective again and again. Recalling his experience in prisons, Vincent remarked:

> Whenever I happened to speak abruptly to the convicts, I spoiled everything. But whenever I praised them for their acceptance and showed them compassion, whenever I sympathized with them in their sorrows, when I kissed their chains and showed how upset I was when they were punished, then they always listened to me and even turned to God. (Abelly, *Life*, p. 183)

Pause: Recall some instance when you were gentle when you could have been angry. Would Christ have been gentle in similar circumstances?

Vincent's Words

Vincent passed on this wisdom about being an effective apostle:

> A missionary needs patience and restraint in his work with those to whom he is sent. The poor whose confes-

sions we hear can be so unrefined, so ignorant and gross. . . . If an individual hasn't the gentleness to put up with their crudeness, what can he hope to accomplish? Nothing at all. On the contrary, he will dishearten these poor ones. When they feel his sharpness, they will be put off and will not return to him to learn those things which are needed for them to be saved. Gentle patience, then, is demanded of us. (*Documents*, vol. 12, p. 305)

In another place, Vincent underlined the same theme:

There are no people more constant and firm in doing good than those who are gentle and gracious. To say the same thing in reverse, those who explode in outrage and allow themselves to be overwhelmed by violent anger are usually more inconsistent because they act only in fits and starts. They are like torrents which are strong and impetuous only when in full flood but which dry up immediately afterwards. But rivers, which symbolize the gentle and gracious, flow on serenely, tranquilly and unfailingly. (*Documents*, vol. 11, p. 65)

Reflection

The Gospels and Epistles frequently remind Christians to be gentle. They should seek to resolve conflicts peacefully, act with kindness, speak courteously—in short, love their neighbors as they love themselves. Such gentleness comes when Christians realize that despite all their sins, God loves them. Secure in the knowledge that "nothing can separate them from the love of God," they can afford to be gentle in the face of hostility, opposition, or indifference.

Christians also need strength. Jesus had to be strong to say and do what he did. Loving, preaching, and healing require courage, energy, ability, and sometimes even righteous anger, the sort of anger Jesus displayed when he drove the money-lenders out of the Temple.

The balance of gentleness and strength is learned in the schools of prayer and experience. Gentleness is not passivity or spinelessness. Strength is not uncontrolled rage or stoic coldness. Determining when to be gentle and when to be forceful should be the subject of our prayerful discernment. When we act, we should learn from our experience, evaluating if our gentleness was cowardice or indifference and if our strength was defensiveness or raw energy.

In short, the apostle must attend carefully to his or her passions, channeling them for good. We are called to be gently strong, and strongly gentle.

✧ Examine relationships or situations in your life in which "gentle patience, then, is demanded of" you. Bring to mind who and what challenges your patient gentleness.

Converse with God about your feelings about these people and situations. Ask God how to be gentle, and also for the graces you need to trust God's love enough to be able to love others even in trying circumstances. If you find yourself irritated and ready to lash out, slow down and pray Vincent's words, "Gentle patience."

✧ Who do you know that best integrates compassion and strength? Think of one person you admire for this balance. Ponder the source of this integration. Thank God for this person, and ask for similar gifts of gentleness and forcefulness.

✧ Does your anger tend to explode, or do you repress it? Converse with Jesus about how to channel this raw energy for good. Ask him how to become so sure of God's unconditional love that exploding or swallowing your anger can be transformed into gentle and strong, active and compassionate love of neighbor.

✧ If your anger has damaged someone's dignity, ask God for mercy and light. And, if it is possible, seek to be reconciled with this person.

✧ When confronted with hostility and opposition, Jesus turned matters over to his Abba and let them go. Meditate on these stories of Jesus' gentle strength:

- ✦ his dispute with the chief priests (Luke 20:1–8)
- ✦ his arrest in the Garden (John 18:1–11)
- ✦ his anointing in Bethany (Mark 14:3–9)
- ✦ his overturning the money-changers' tables (Matthew 21:12–13)
- ✦ his challenge to Herod (Luke 13:31–35)
- ✦ his confrontation with the Pharisees and lawyers (Luke 11:37–53)

God's Word

Shoulder my yoke and learn from me, for I am gentle and humble in heart. (Matthew 11:29)

Rekindle the gift of God that is within you through the laying on of my hands; for God did not give us a spirit of cowardice, but rather a spirit of power and of love and of self-discipline. . . . Join with me in bearing hardships for the gospel, relying on the power of God, who saved us and called us with a holy calling. (Adapted from 2 Timothy 1:6–10)

Closing prayer:

My God,
>in order to please you
>I desire with all my heart
>to be respectful and gentle towards my neighbor. . . .

I beg you, my God,
>in the name of Jesus, your beloved Son,
>who is gentleness and love personified,
>to grant me your assistance,
>so that, by your grace,
>I shall never consciously act without gentleness.
>>(Braakhuis, *Praying*, no. 6)

✧ **Meditation 14** ✧

Creativity and Cooperation in Ministry

Theme: Announcing the Good News to poor people calls for ingenuity combined with teamwork. The way Jesus set new courses and gathered the Apostles together served as Vincent's example of how to be creative and pull people together.

Opening prayer: Creator, expand my vision and fire my creativity in the service of your Reign. Draw me together with other Christians who seek to serve your people. Lead us peacefully on your way through all the tensions and pressures of our work together.

About Vincent

Vincent sought to focus all of his effort on the direct service of poor people. However, he knew that to do so, he would need to gather, motivate, and negotiate with diverse groups of people. Vincent constantly devised ingenious ways to pool the talents of willing workers.

His creativity manifested itself even in the recognition of potential helpers. He tapped assistance, skills, or talent from socialites, politicians, professors, jailers, military officers, wives, prisoners, farm laborers, merchants, parish priests, and cloistered nuns. One example of his creative recruitment was Margaret Naseau, a young peasant woman. Vincent included her in a confraternity of wealthy aristocrats that he had gathered in Paris to do works of charity. She certainly did not fit the profile of the group. They came from the elite; Margaret was an unlettered milkmaid.

However, in her desire to educate poor folk, Margaret had taught herself to read by asking passersby the meaning of the different letters of the alphabet. When she heard that poor and sick people were being treated in a Parisian parish, she showed up at its front door and volunteered to care for them. Unlike the high-born women, she understood the needs and condition of the poor and sick. Gradually, Margaret became the mainstay of the confraternity and attracted other farm women to the ministry. One cold night, she took in a homeless girl who, as it turned out, had the plague. Margaret caught the contagion and soon died. In his talks, Vincent often used Margaret's life as a model of perfect service to poor people.

Vincent's own creativity is illustrated by his appreciation of someone of Margaret's abilities, and even more so by his involvement of Louise de Marillac. Louise assumed direction of the confraternity, nourished it, and organized it into the community known universally as the Daughters of Charity.

Before Vincent, no one had thought that "simple country girls" (Vincent's words) could do pastoral ministry. Even more radical was the notion of vowed women working outside the cloister. Seeing the Daughters of Charity out in the slums and city streets raised many eyebrows. Vincent staunchly defended his innovation. If God's poor and sick people needed ministering to, creative adaptations had to be made. He remarked:

> Since they (the Daughters of Charity) are more exposed in these places than nuns, usually having only the houses of the sick as their convent, a rented room as their cell, the parish church as their chapel, the city streets or hospital wards as their cloister, obedience as their enclosure, the fear of God as the bars on their windows, modesty as their veil, confidence in Providence as their profession,
> . . . they are required to lead a life as filled with virtue as

if they were professed in some religious order. Because of all this, they are to behave wherever they might be in the world with as much recollection, purity of heart and body, detachment from possessions and good example as real nuns in the seclusion of a convent. (*Documents*, vol. 10, p. 661)

Using traditional terminology, Vincent explained the unique, creative form of life the Daughters of Charity developed. With characteristic imagination, Vincent had recruited one more underutilized group into his ever-widening circle of evangelizers and ministers of poor people.

Pause: Ask yourself: Have I sometimes held on to comfortable ways of serving other people when newer ways would have been more helpful?

Vincent's Words

Encouraging one of his communities to overcome obstacles to their ministry, Vincent said, "Love is inventive, even to infinity" (*Documents*, vol. 11, p. 146).

Love must also foster cooperation in ministry. In a directive to his priests, Vincent reminded them of the motivation of their work together:

Christ, our Savior, formed apostles and disciples into a community and gave them guidelines for getting along well with each other. . . . Our little Congregation wants to follow in the footsteps of Christ and the disciples. (*Constitutions*, p. 129)

Finally, Vincent reminded the women in one of the charitable organizations he founded that it is divine providence that calls Christians to be creative in forming communities of service:

It has been eight hundred years now since women have had any public role in the Church. In early times there were deaconesses who oversaw the women of the congregation and instructed them in the ceremonies then in use.

. . . But in the time of Charlemagne, because of some unknown design of Providence, this custom stopped and
your sex was deprived of providing all these kinds of services. In our day, however, this same Providence prompt-
ed you to take up the crucial work of caring for poor
people suffering in the hospitals. A few women responded to these promptings and after a while were joined by
others to form an association. God has given them as
mothers to the abandoned children who are sick in the
hospitals. In Paris, they are called upon to dispense many
alms. . . . By the grace of God, these good women have
responded to these needs with great warmth and steadi-
ness. (*Documents*, vol. 10, pp. 809–810)

Reflection

Vincent's legacy is a mixture of single-mindedness and open-
ness. With his heart set on loving God and neighbor, Vincent
searched for whatever methods might make that love active
and credible. Approaches that escaped other people's attention caught his eye because of their apostolic potential.

Staying focused on service allowed Vincent to loosen his
grip on what he already knew. After deliberating, he would
step out beyond the tried and true when he saw a need to be
met or good to be done. For example, he innovated by estab-
lishing the confraternities of rich people working with poor
ones, caring for beggars in halfway houses, getting prisoners
to help other prisoners during missions, giving retreats to
gatherings of priests, organizing women to minister in people's homes, and so on.

Simultaneously, Vincent always encouraged cooperation
among people in service. Jesus gathered the apostles and disciples together so that the Good News could go out to distant
lands. Vincent followed Jesus' example, and he used his creative abilities to gather, direct, and encourage cooperation and
mutual support in ministry.

Even if he ruffled the feathers of powerful figures, service
of the poor took precedence. Vincent willingly changed his
own habits if they obstructed his mission and challenged the

narrow thinking of other people. Vincent stayed constant in his ends, but flexible in his means. The love of Christ provided his anchor and his freedom to do what needed to be done.

✧ Pray repeatedly Vincent's words: "Love is inventive." Attend to any images that come to mind as you pray.

When you feel ready, recall an instance when you felt at a dead end in your attempts to love someone. Then ponder these questions:

◆ Did my love draw me to seek means or approaches that were out of the ordinary for me?
◆ What were my feelings?
◆ If I did not try other approaches, why not?
◆ Is there anyone that I want to love right now who thwarts my attempts?
◆ How can I let my love be inventive? [You might even list ways of approaching this person; brainstorm.]

Thank God for creativity in the past, and ask God for the graces that you need right now to love creatively.

✧ On many occasions, Jesus acted independently of the expected way of doing things. After relaxing your body and breathing slowly and deeply, meditate on this story of Jesus confronting the scribes and Pharisees when they objected to curing on the Sabbath:

> One Sabbath Jesus started teaching in the synagogue. One of the men present had a withered right hand. Jesus knew that the scribes and Pharisees were spying on him to see if he would actually cure someone on the Sabbath. They hankered after a charge to level at Jesus. Even knowing what they were up to, Jesus beckoned to the man with the withered hand and said, "Stand in the middle of the synagogue." The man did so.
>
> Jesus then asked the scribes and Pharisees, "I ask you: is it lawful to do good or to do evil on the Sabbath? To save life, or to destroy it?" Jesus stared at them, then said to the man, "Hold out your hand." When he did so, the hand had been cured. The scribes and Pharisees were furious and talked about how to cope with Jesus.
>
> (Adapted from Luke 6:6–11)

Now reflect on these questions:

✦ As you read the passage, what feelings ran through you?

✦ Was Jesus too hard on the scribes and Pharisees? If so, why?

✦ Have you ever let tradition, peer pressure, or custom dictate the terms or ways of love or charity? Examine your consciousness on this question.

Talk with Jesus about your own attitude toward social norms, custom, and law when they come into conflict with love.

✧ Cooperation in ministry can be fraught with difficulties, both major and minor. In your journal, dialog with Jesus about a situation that you find most perplexing right now. In the conversation, be sure to ask Jesus to show you ways in which you can create better cooperation or at least break the tension. Pray for the graces you need to be Christlike in this situation.

✧ Reflect on Vincent's remarks to the women of the confraternity. Ponder their significance for women and men in ministry today. Then reflect on Paul's words to the Galatians: "There can be neither Jew nor Greek, there can be neither slave nor free, there can be neither male nor female; for you are all one in Christ Jesus" (3:28).

Pray this phrase repeatedly in spare moments during the day: "All are one in Christ."

✧ Is there some need in your family, parish, or neighborhood that wants for attention? Can you gather people together to solve this problem? Pray for whatever help you need from God to take action.

God's Word

Above all, clothe yourselves with love, which binds everything together in perfect harmony. And let the peace of Christ rule in your hearts, to which indeed you were called in the one body. And be thankful. Let the word of

Christ dwell in you richly; teach and admonish one another in all wisdom. . . . And whatever you do, in word
or deed, do everything in the name of . . . Jesus, giving
thanks to God . . . through him. (Adapted from Colossians 3:14–17)

Closing prayer:

> O my God,
> > may it please you to be the bond
> > which ties the hearts of evangelizers together
> > in a common attitude of humility,
> > of unity, and of respect for one another. . . .
>
> Let the good effects of their mutual affection,
> > which you allow to develop among them,
> > steadily grow and flourish,
> > and make the fruits of their labors
> > for the salvation of souls
> > constantly increase.
>
> Strengthen them in their . . . efforts,
> > and be yourself their ultimate reward.
> > > > > > (Braakhuis, *Praying*, no. 28)

Contemplation and Action

Theme: For our ministry to continue during the rough spots, and to be done according to God's will, it has to be grounded in prayer and contemplation. Vincent models the necessary balance between contemplation and action.

Opening prayer: God of goodness, you hold all things together. Let my prayer anchor my action, and my action nourish my prayer. In everything, may I attend to you with all my heart.

About Vincent

One Sunday during his homily, Vincent alerted his rural congregation that a single mother and her children in the area were all sick and close to starvation. That afternoon, parishioners streamed into the family's hut bringing medicine and meals. Later in the week when Vincent came to visit, he found the hut filled with unwashed clothes and rotting food. The Sunday help had been real, but only stopgap. After thinking and praying about it, Vincent set up a system to provide long-term assistance. He even wrote a how-to manual for setting up a parish-based aid society. Many districts adopted the plan and called their societies the Confraternities of Charity. The parishioners' charity to the poor woman and her children was good, but because it was done without sufficient reflection, it lacked wisdom and practicality for the long term.

The action led to reflection, and Vincent's plans then profited from his meditation and prayer. Prayer not only informed action, but as time went on, Vincent understood more plainly that encounters with poor people were encounters with Jesus Christ. He would speak of the complementarity between seeking God in prayer and finding God in compassionate action. Vincent vividly expressed this complementary nature in his talks with the Daughters of Charity.

Pressed by tasks that could not wait, many Daughters found themselves fighting the clock to balance prayer and work. Vincent told them:

> If at the time for prayer in the morning, you have to bring medicine to your patients, do it peacefully . . . Give yourself over to God's will, offer up what you are about to do, join your intention with the prayer that is being made back at home, and go about your task with a clear conscience.
>
> If, when you return, you are free to spend a little time at prayer, all well and good. But you must not worry yourself or think you have failed to keep the rule if you omit that prayer time. It is not lost when you leave it for a good reason. And, my dear daughters, if there ever was a good reason, it is service of the poor. To leave God for God, that is, to leave one work of God to do another of greater obligation (or merit), is not to leave God. For example, you leave prayer or spiritual reading, or you go against your rule of silence to help a poor person. The truth is, my daughters, that to give help in this instance is to observe the rules! What a great comfort for a good Daughter of Charity to be able to say to herself: "I am going to help my sick poor, but God will receive this action instead of the prayer I should be making just now." Then she goes off happily to wherever God calls her. (*Documents*, vol. 9, p. 319)

Pause: Reflect on your own experience of the interchange between prayer and action. Have they mutually reinforced one another?

Vincent's Words

Vincent pinpoints a privileged source of contemplation:

> We have to make our occupations holy. We do this by seeking God in them. We do our work to find God in it rather than to just get it done. (*Documents*, vol. 12, p. 132)

In the rule of life Vincent proposed for the Daughters of Charity, he insisted that Jesus should be the guiding example for how prayer and action are integrated:

> [Jesus is] so perfect a model. . . . [The Daughters are directed to] strive to live in a holy manner, and labor with great care to attain perfection; uniting the exercise of a spiritual life with the exterior duties of Christian charity toward the poor, according to the present Rules, which they will endeavor to practice with great fidelity, as the surest means of attaining this end. (Ignatius Melito, "St. Vincent's Legacy," *Vincentian Heritage* 2 [1981]: 5)

Finally, in this famous line, Vincent told his community:

> Give me a man of prayer and he will be capable of anything. He may say with the apostle, "I can do all things in him who strengthens me." (*Documents*, vol. 11, p. 83)

Reflection

When Vincent speaks of action, he means effort for the Reign of God. This effort is the overflowing of grace, a free response to the Gospel's call to love our neighbor. Action stands in sharp contrast to mere activity, which may *seem* like zeal but is so compulsive or rootless that it withers under the hot sun of apostolic demands.

Analogously, prayer and contemplation are open to everything that God is doing in the world; they are long, loving, vulnerable looks at God's manifold presence in creation. On the other hand, people can think that they are praying, but if prayer is disconnected from the wider world, it turns into a caricature of itself. Prayer not rooted in God's presence in experience can be form without substance.

Prayer, contemplation, and action vitalize each other. When God guides and graces our action, that action becomes a prayer and a source of contemplation. When our prayer and contemplation truly examine the reality of God's presence in the sufferings and joys, dangers and celebrations in the world, they flower into charity in action.

✧ Pray these words of Vincent slowly and meditatively: "Give yourself over to God's will, offer up what you are about to do." Then share with God those times when you felt that what you were doing was God's will, and that God was working with you.

To remind yourself of God's presence as you work— whether washing laundry, fixing a muffler, giving an injection, keeping accounts—offer Vincent's prayer during the day. Deliberately offer "what you are about to do" to God.

✧ Many times life becomes frantic with activity. Recall a recent day when you felt unrooted, distracted. What was the quality of your interaction with people? Looking back, how much good did you really accomplish by all that activity? Would some of it have been avoidable or better directed? In prayer, ask God for the graces you need to relate with people and to act with careful attentiveness.

✧ Vincent gave the Daughters of Charity a guideline for their action: "To leave God for God; that is, to leave one work of God to do another of greater obligation (or merit), is not to leave God." How might you put this wisdom to use in your daily life?

✧ While sometimes just resting in God's presence is desirable and necessary, at other times making our experience the subject or content of our prayer is, also. Traditionally, four ways of praying have been described: *lectio, meditatio, oratio,* and *contemplatio.* Bring some significant experience (an argument, a decision, an encounter, an accomplishment) to your prayer now and use each method to pray your experience:

✦ *Lectio:* Reflect on passages from the Bible that speak to this experience. Read it with an open heart. Perhaps write your reflections in your journal.

✦ *Meditatio:* Dialog with Jesus about the experience. Remember that sometimes in dialog you have to wait patiently for the other person to respond. This dialog meditation may be written too.

✦ *Oratio:* Offer prayers of praise, thanksgiving, petition, and contrition in regard to this experience.

✦ *Contemplatio:* Offer this experience to God. Then, sit quietly, listening to what God might say, resting in God's presence, silent, attentive.

✧ Is your prayer too narrow or too small? Are your concerns almost totally private or generically wide? Does your prayer include concern for justice, peace, world hunger—the big issues, as well as desire for healing, thanks for gifts, and so on? How can you strengthen your belief that prayer is powerful?

God's Word

God commands that we believe in the name of Jesus Christ and that we love one another. All who obey God's commandments dwell in God, and God dwells in them. We know that God lives in us because of the Spirit that God has sent to us. (Adapted from 1 John 3:23–24)

Closing prayer:

This is my prayer to you, O Lord! Give to me your special favor. Pour out your truth and mercy on me in an abundance that will enable me to put your love into practice, filling me with true affection for you, for my neighbor, and also for myself. (*Documents*, vol. 10, pp. 474–475)

S·E·N·T

✧ For Further Reading ✧

Braakhuis, Frits (Frederick), trans. *Praying in St. Vincent's Spirit*. Hugh O'Donnell and Jay Gibson, eds. Denver: St. Thomas Theological Seminary, 1990.

Calvet, Jean. *Saint Vincent de Paul*. Trans. Lancelot C. Sheppard. New York: David McKay Co., 1951.

Cognet, Louis and Leonard von Matt. *St. Vincent de Paul*. Trans. Emma Craufurd. Chicago: Henry Regnery Co., 1960.

Coste, Pierre. *The Life and Works of St. Vincent de Paul*. 3 vols. Trans. Joseph Leonard. New York: New City Press, 1987.

Cristiani, Leon. *St. Vincent de Paul*. Trans. John Gregoli. Boston: St. Paul Editions, 1977.

Dodin, Andre. *Vincent de Paul and Charity: A Contemporary Portrait of His Life and Apostolic Activity*. Trans. Jean Marie Smith and Dennis Saunders. New Rochelle, NY: New City Press, 1993.

Leonard, Joseph. *St. Vincent de Paul and Mental Prayer*. London: Burns, Oates, and Washbourne, 1925.

Maloney, Robert. *The Way of Vincent de Paul: A Contemporary Spirituality in the Service of the Poor*. New York: New City Press, 1992.

Maynard, Abbe Michel Ulysse. *Virtues and Spiritual Doctrine of St. Vincent de Paul*. Trans. Carlton Prindeville. Saint Louis: Vincentian Foreign Mission Press, 1961.

Mezzadri, Luigi. *A Short Life of St. Vincent de Paul*. Trans. Thomas Davitt. Dublin, Ireland: The Columba Press, 1992.

Purcell, Mary. *The World of Monsieur Vincent*. Chicago: Loyola University Press, 1989.

Acknowledgments (*continued*)

The scriptural material found on pages 38, 40, 50, 62, 76, 85, 87–88, 93, 100 (second excerpt), 105, 107, and 110 is freely adapted and is not to be understood or used as an official translation of the Bible.

All other scriptural quotations used in this book are from the New Jerusalem Bible. Copyright © 1985 by Darton, Longman & Todd, London; and Doubleday, a division of Bantam, Doubleday, Dell Publishing Group, New York. Used with permission.

The excerpt on page 31 is from *The Life and Works of Saint Vincent de Paul*, by Pierre Coste, translated by Joseph Leonard (Westminster, MD: The Newman Press, 1952), volume 3, page 365.

The excerpt on page 33 is from *The God Who Fell From Heaven*, by John Shea (Allen, TX: Argus Communications, 1979), page 7.

The excerpts on pages 36, 47 (second excerpt), 64–65, 69–70 (second and third excerpts), 80, 91 (second excerpt), and 103 (second excerpt) are from Vincent de Paul's *Common Rules*, as they appeared in *Constitutions and Statutes of the Congregation of the Mission*, by the General Curia of the Congregation of the Mission (Rome: 1984, English translation in Philadelphia: 1989), pages 108–112, 108, 150, 105–110, 109, 157, and 129, respectively.

The excerpts on page 42 are from *The Life and Works of Saint Vincent de Paul*, by Pierre Coste, translated by Joseph Leonard (Westminster, MD: The Newman Press, 1952), volume 1, pages 355 and 299, respectively.

The excerpts on pages 51, 72 (third excerpt), 78 (second excerpt), 94, 100 (third excerpt), and 107 (second excerpt), are from *Praying in St. Vincent's Spirit*, translated by Frits J. Braakhuis, edited by Hugh O'Donnel, and Jay Gibson (Denver: Saint Thomas Theological Seminary, 1990), numbers 17, 7, 19, 29, 6, and 28, respectively.

The excerpts on page 59 are from *The Life and Works of Saint Vincent de Paul*, by Pierre Coste, translated by Joseph Leonard (Westminster, MD: The Newman Press, 1952), volume 2, pages 267 and 322, respectively.

The excerpts on pages 69 (first excerpt) and 96 (second excerpt) are from *La Vie du Venerable Serviteur de Dieu Vincent de Paul*, by Louis Abelly (Paris: Florentin Lambert, 1664), pages 177–178 and 183, respectively.

The excerpt on page 71 is from *Markings*, by Dag Hammarskjöld, translated by Leif Sjöberg and W. H. Auden (London: Faber and Faber, 1964), page 15.

The second excerpt on page 72 is from *The Cost of Discipleship*, by Dietrich Bonhoeffer (New York: Macmillan Paperbacks, 1963), page 37.

The second excerpt on page 110 is from "Saint Vincent's Legacy" by Ignatius Melito, *Vincentian Heritage*, volume 2, 1981, page 5.

Titles in the Companions for the Journey Series

Praying with Catherine of Siena

Praying with Clare of Assisi   *Available fall 1994*

Praying with Dominic

Praying with Dorothy Day   *Available spring 1995*

Praying with Elizabeth Seton

Praying with Francis of Assisi

Praying with Hildegard of Bingen

Praying with Ignatius of Loyola

Praying with John Baptist de La Salle

Praying with John of the Cross

Praying with Julian of Norwich

Praying with Teresa of Ávila

Praying with Thérèse of Lisieux

Praying with Thomas Merton

Praying with Vincent de Paul

Order from your local religious bookstore or from

Saint Mary's Press
702 TERRACE HEIGHTS
WINONA MN 55987-1320
USA